Ending Homelessness By 2035: A Blueprint for Change in America.

Unlocking the Power of Community and Policy to Resolve America's Most Pressing Issue, Now.

John Whitfield

Table of Contents

Preface 3

Chapter 1: Beyond Shelter: The Broader Impacts of Addressing Homelessness 5

Chapter 2: Dispelling Myths: Homelessness and Personal Failure 14

Chapter 3: The Economics of Inaction: Why We Can't Afford to Ignore Homelessness 23

Chapter 4: Housing First: A Foundation for Stability 32

Chapter 5: Economic Safety Nets: Preventing Homelessness Through Job Security 42

Chapter 6: Building Solutions: Making Affordable Housing Accessible 51

Chapter 7: Integrating Health: The Role of Mental Care and Addiction Treatment 61

Chapter 8: Power in Unity: Community Engagement in Homelessness Programs 72

Chapter 9: Flexible Frameworks: Adapting Strategies to Local Needs 81

Chapter 10: The Power of Data: Making Informed Adjustments for Long-term Success 91

Conclusion: 102

Epilogue 104

Preface

"The only way to see the limits of the possible is to go beyond them into the impossible." – Arthur C. Clarke

Imagine a world where every individual has a place they can call home—a sanctuary where they can retreat, rejuvenate, and reconnect with their dreams. This vision, although seemingly utopian, encapsulates the essence of what we aim to achieve: **ending homelessness in America by 2035**.

This book is crafted as a comprehensive blueprint that addresses the daunting challenge of homelessness. It delves into the systemic causes, financial implications, and viable strategies necessary for crafting effective solutions. With meticulous research and heartfelt narratives, the book paints a vivid picture of the current landscape and charts a clear path forward.

I was inspired to write this book after witnessing the transformative power of community efforts in several towns where local leaders and citizens came together to tackle this issue head-on. Their success stories, fueled by compassion and innovation, convinced me that with the right approach, ending homelessness is within our reach.

One such encounter involved meeting Maria, a community organizer who transformed an abandoned lot into a thriving hub for temporary housing and skill development. Her story is a testament to what can be achieved when communities rally together to support their most vulnerable members. It is these real-world examples that I bring to you, woven through the narrative to demonstrate that change is not only necessary but entirely feasible.

Throughout this journey, I've been fortunate to draw inspiration from various sources—ranging from academic research and policy analyses to boots-on-the-ground experiences shared by subject matter experts, community activists and volunteers. Their insights have been invaluable in shaping the perspectives and solutions presented in this book.

I extend my deepest gratitude to you for choosing to engage with this work. Your commitment to exploring these pages signals a shared belief in our collective ability to foster significant social change. This book is intended for policymakers, community leaders, activists, students, and anyone who believes in the power of informed action and compassionate leadership. No prior expertise is required—just an open heart and a willing mind.

As you turn each page, I invite you to envision the role you can play in reshaping our society. Together, through informed policy-making and robust community engagement, we can transform the landscape of homelessness. Your journey through this book is not just about understanding a societal issue but about equipping yourself with the knowledge and tools to be part of a lasting solution.

Thank you once again for your time and dedication. Let's embark on this path toward change together, armed with hope and driven by purpose.

Chapter 1:
Beyond Shelter: The Broader Impacts of Addressing Homelessness

On a brisk autumn morning, the city awakens with a gentle sigh, its streets shaded by the golden hues of early sunlight filtering through the sparse leaves of aging oaks. Amid this quiet awakening, Michael stands outside a newly inaugurated shelter for the homeless, his breath visible in the cool air. The sharp scent of rain from last night's downpour mingles with the earthy aroma of wet pavement.

Michael watches as individuals, some hesitant and others more assured, make their way into the facility. Each person carries not just their physical burdens but also an invisible load of experiences and hardships. Michael knows their stories well; he's spent months organizing community support and resources to make this project a reality. The sight fills him with a mixture of pride and worry—pride for what has been accomplished, worry for what might still fail.

He remembers sitting across from Anna during one of their planning meetings. She had lost her job during a wave of layoffs that hit her industry hard—a story not uncommon in recent times. "It's not just about getting a roof over our heads," she had said, stirring her coffee slowly, eyes not meeting his. "It's about feeling safe again... feeling like part of society." Her words had stuck with him, shaping his resolve.

Now, as he steps inside the shelter, he is greeted by warm smiles and nods from volunteers setting up for breakfast service. The clatter of utensils and plates forms a backdrop to his thoughts. The air is filled with smells of coffee and toasted bread—simple comforts that seem to momentarily lift everyone's spirits.

Michael pauses by a window overlooking the small garden at the back where several residents help tend vegetables and herbs—a small initiative to instill responsibility and foster community spirit among them. He thinks about how solutions like these extend beyond mere shelter; they are stepping stones toward societal equality and enhanced public health.

The day stretches ahead filled with meetings, discussions on future projects, and securing funds, all mundane but crucial tasks that keep such initiatives alive. As Michael prepares to step into another meeting room filled with potential donors, he wonders whether enough people realize how intertwined homelessness is with broader societal issues—how solving it could mean uplifting entire communities economically and socially.

How many more shelters would it take before society at large understands that addressing homelessness transcends providing mere shelter?

Unveiling the Ripple Effect: How Solving Homelessness Transforms Society

Addressing homelessness is not merely about providing roofs over heads; it's a powerful catalyst for societal transformation. This chapter explores the profound impacts that resolving homelessness has on public health, economic vitality, and social equality. By weaving together a tapestry of evidence-based strategies and heartening success stories, we paint a comprehensive picture of how holistic solutions to homelessness can extend benefits far beyond the individuals directly affected.

Homelessness is more than just a lack of physical shelter; it is a complex socio-economic issue that affects all of us in one way or another. Public health systems, for instance, are significantly strained by the high needs of homeless populations, who are more susceptible to acute and chronic illnesses and often rely on emergency services for care. By finding sustainable housing solutions, we can alleviate these pressures and improve health outcomes not just for the homeless but for entire communities.

Economic Impacts: More Than Just Dollars Saved

Economically, reducing homelessness can lead to enhanced productivity and reduced public expenditure. When people have stable housing, they are better able to find and retain jobs, contributing positively to the economy. Furthermore, less money is required for emergency healthcare services, law enforcement involvement, and social welfare programs when fewer people are homeless. This chapter will delve into how cities that have successfully reduced homelessness reap economic benefits that far exceed the costs of the programs implemented.

Social inequalities are also intricately linked with homelessness. Often, those who fall into homelessness come from marginalized communities or have faced significant life adversities. Addressing homelessness can thus be seen as a critical step towards social justice, providing opportunities for empowerment and breaking cycles of poverty and exclusion.

Envisioning a Future Without Homelessness

The broader societal implications of solving homelessness underscore the importance of strategic, coordinated actions. It's about creating systemic changes that not only provide immediate relief but also dismantle the underlying structures that perpetuate homelessness. This involves comprehensive policy reforms, community engagement, and continuous advocacy to ensure that everyone has access to adequate housing.

Throughout this book, we aim to equip you with a detailed roadmap for eradicating homelessness by 2035. Each chapter builds on this foundational understanding by offering specific strategies tailored to different aspects of the issue—from understanding systemic causes to implementing effective interventions. By fostering a deeper understanding of both the challenges and potential solutions, we empower policymakers, activists, and concerned citizens alike to take meaningful action.

By approaching homelessness as a multifaceted problem with wide-reaching implications, we can mobilize a broader coalition of stakeholders invested in its resolution. Each section in this chapter sets up critical learning objectives that will help us explore how interconnected public systems are improved when we address this pressing issue effectively.

In engaging with these themes, readers will gain insights into how resolving homelessness does not merely change lives—it revitalizes entire communities. Let us embark on this enlightening journey together, exploring how targeted actions today can pave the way for a more inclusive and prosperous tomorrow.

Addressing homelessness goes beyond providing shelter; it has a profound impact on public health systems as well. When individuals have stable housing, they are more likely to access and adhere to medical treatment, leading to better health outcomes. **Homelessness resolution can alleviate the burden on emergency rooms and hospitals**, where those without homes often seek care for preventable conditions that have escalated due to lack of proper treatment. By reducing the number of homeless individuals, we can free up resources within the healthcare system to focus on proactive care rather than reactive interventions.

Moreover, homelessness resolution contributes to **improved mental health outcomes**. The stress and uncertainty of living without a stable home can exacerbate existing mental health conditions or lead to the development of new ones. By providing housing stability, individuals can focus on their mental well-being, leading to better overall health outcomes and reduced strain on mental health services.

Substance abuse disorders are also closely linked with homelessness. Individuals experiencing homelessness are more vulnerable to substance abuse as a coping mechanism for their circumstances. By addressing homelessness and providing support services, we can help individuals overcome substance abuse challenges and reduce the strain on addiction treatment programs.

Furthermore, **homelessness is intertwined with infectious disease transmission**. Living in crowded shelters or on the streets increases the risk of exposure to communicable diseases such as tuberculosis or influenza. Addressing homelessness not only provides individuals with safer living conditions but also contributes to public health by reducing the spread of infectious diseases within communities.

Join me as we delve deeper into how resolving homelessness impacts our public health systems.

Addressing homelessness goes beyond providing shelter; it also holds significant economic benefits for society as a whole. When individuals are lifted out of homelessness, it not only improves their personal well-being but also contributes to the overall economic prosperity of a community. **Reducing homelessness leads to a ripple effect that positively impacts various sectors and ultimately boosts the economy.**

One key economic benefit of reducing homelessness is the **cost savings** for both local governments and taxpayers. Homelessness places a significant financial burden on communities through emergency room visits, law enforcement interactions, and temporary shelter costs. By providing stable housing and support services, communities can lower these expenses and allocate resources more efficiently. **Investing in solutions to homelessness is not just a moral imperative but also a smart financial decision.**

Moreover, addressing homelessness **increases productivity** within the workforce. When individuals have stable housing, they are better able to secure and maintain employment. Stable housing provides the foundation for individuals to focus on their work, pursue education or training opportunities, and contribute meaningfully to the economy. **Reducing homelessness translates into a more robust and engaged workforce**, benefiting businesses and the overall economy.

Another economic benefit of resolving homelessness is the **boost to local businesses**. Stable housing allows individuals to become active participants in their communities, supporting local businesses through increased consumer spending. When individuals have a place to call home, they are more likely to invest in their surroundings, frequent local establishments, and contribute to the economic vitality of their neighborhoods.

Furthermore, addressing homelessness can lead to **long-term economic growth** by breaking the cycle of poverty for individuals and families. Stable housing creates a platform for individuals to plan for their future, pursue educational opportunities, and secure better employment prospects. By investing in solutions to homelessness, communities can uplift marginalized populations and create a more equitable society where everyone has the opportunity to thrive economically.

In conclusion, reducing homelessness is not just a social responsibility but also an economic imperative. By investing in solutions that provide stable housing and support services for those experiencing homelessness, communities can unlock numerous economic benefits that contribute to overall prosperity. **The economic advantages of addressing homelessness extend far beyond individual circumstances; they have the power to transform communities and drive sustainable growth for society as a whole**.

Addressing homelessness is not just about providing shelter; it is a crucial step towards reducing social inequalities. **By resolving homelessness, we can work towards creating a more equitable society where everyone has the opportunity to thrive**. Homelessness is often intertwined with systemic issues such as poverty, lack of affordable housing, and limited access to resources. **When we tackle homelessness, we are also addressing these underlying factors that contribute to social disparities**.

Reducing social inequalities through homelessness resolution involves creating pathways for marginalized individuals to access resources and opportunities. Homeless individuals face significant barriers to education, employment, and healthcare, perpetuating a cycle of poverty and exclusion. By providing stable housing and support services, we can empower individuals to rebuild their lives and reintegrate into society. **This not only benefits those directly affected by homelessness but also contributes to a more inclusive and cohesive community**.

Homelessness disproportionately affects vulnerable populations, including minorities, LGBTQ individuals, veterans, and those with disabilities. By prioritizing efforts to end homelessness, we are taking a stand against discrimination and marginalization. **We are sending a powerful message that everyone deserves dignity, respect, and equal opportunities**. When we address the root causes of homelessness and provide tailored support to those in need, we are fostering a more compassionate and empathetic society.

Reducing social inequalities through homelessness resolution is a multifaceted approach that requires collaboration across sectors. It involves not only providing housing but also addressing issues such as healthcare access, mental health support, job training, and community integration. **By working together towards a common goal of ending homelessness**, we can create a more level playing field where everyone has the chance to succeed.

When we prioritize resolving homelessness as a means to reduce social inequalities, we are investing in the well-being of our entire community. **By lifting up the most vulnerable among us**, we are building a stronger and more resilient society for all. **Every individual deserves the opportunity to live with dignity and purpose**, and by coming together to address homelessness, we can make this vision a reality for everyone.

Addressing homelessness is far more than a humanitarian effort; it's an investment in our collective future. By weaving together the threads of public health, economic stability, and social equity, we create a stronger, more resilient society. This first chapter has laid a robust foundation, revealing how comprehensive solutions to homelessness extend well beyond the provision of shelter.

Public health systems thrive when homelessness is mitigated. Reduced strain on emergency services and hospitals is a direct benefit, but the ripple effects extend further, enhancing community health and reducing overall healthcare costs. This isn't just theory; it's a reflection of a healthier society where every individual has the chance to lead a productive, fulfilling life.

Economic benefits are undeniable. Think of it as unlocking potential. Every individual housed and supported translates into a participant in our economy, not merely a bystander. Employment rises, consumption increases, and public expenditures decrease. This cycle of positive economic activity fosters a more dynamic market environment benefiting everyone.

Reducing social inequalities is perhaps the most profound impact. Ensuring that everyone has access to basic necessities like housing is a powerful equalizer. It breaks down barriers, builds bridges across societal divides, and fosters a sense of community and shared responsibility. When the playing field is leveled, talent and determination, not circumstance, dictate one's path.

As we progress through this book, we'll explore specific strategies and real-world examples that not only support these points but also illustrate the transformative effects of such policies. Each subsequent chapter builds on this narrative, outlining clear, actionable steps that can be taken to end homelessness by 2035.

By turning these pages, you are joining a movement towards not just resolving an issue but also empowering a nation. The insights here are designed not only to inform but to inspire action and instill hope. Your engagement and understanding are crucial as we move forward, shaping policies and community efforts that reflect our shared values and aspirations for a society where no individual lacks a place to call home.

Together, let's envision and work towards a future where addressing homelessness with thoughtful, comprehensive strategies creates waves of positive change across all sectors of society. Your continued interest and involvement are vital as we delve deeper into this critical issue, exploring innovative solutions and celebrating the successes along the way. Let's embrace this journey with optimism and determination, recognizing that every step taken is a step toward a better tomorrow for all.

Chapter 2: Dispelling Myths: Homelessness and Personal Failure

In the dim light of early morning, Thomas stood at the corner of a bustling city street, his breath visible in the chill air. He watched as people hurried by, their faces set against the cold, their eyes fixed ahead. Thomas felt a pang of something akin to envy; they seemed to belong somewhere, to someone.

He turned his attention back to the small cart filled with newspapers he was supposed to sell. The papers were stacked neatly, their headlines screaming of crises and controversies. Yet buried beneath those loud declarations were smaller stories about city council plans for new homeless shelters and affordable housing initiatives—policies meant to address problems like his own.

Thomas remembered the days before he found himself without a roof over his head. He had been a carpenter, proud of his skill in turning raw wood into something beautiful and functional. But an injury left him unable to work, and medical bills piled up quickly. The descent into homelessness felt both swift and gradual, a slide that seemed both inevitable yet preventable in hindsight.

A young woman approached the cart, her scarf pulled up against her face. She bought a paper without meeting his eyes. Thomas watched her as she walked away, blending into the crowd. He thought about how easy it was for people to overlook what they did not wish to see: men and women like him who had slipped through cracks widened by systemic failures.

As he handed out newspapers throughout the day, Thomas's mind wandered over what could be done differently. It wasn't just about more shelters or feeding programs; it was about understanding why people ended up on the streets in the first place. It was about policies that recognized and addressed issues like healthcare access, affordable housing shortages, and job training, policies that could help prevent others from ending up where he was now.

The sun dipped lower in the sky, casting long shadows between buildings as Thomas packed up his unsold newspapers. He felt weary but restless with thoughts swirling around potential solutions that seemed just out of reach, a societal shift towards empathy and action rather than judgment and neglect.

How might we shift our perceptions to foster policies that not only recognize but actively address the complex roots of homelessness?

Is Homelessness a Mirror of Personal Failure or a Reflection of Societal Flaws?

Homelessness is often viewed through the lens of personal inadequacy, a narrative deeply ingrained in the fabric of societal perception. This chapter aims to dismantle that notion, arguing that homelessness is not predominantly a result of individual failings but rather a complex interplay of systemic issues. By understanding this, we can shift our approach towards solutions that are not only compassionate but also effective.

Unveiling the Stigma

The stigma attached to homelessness is pervasive and damaging. It paints those experiencing homelessness as architects of their own misfortune, which simplifies and distorts reality. This chapter will explore how such stigmatization not only affects those it targets but also skews public opinion and policy-making against meaningful, systemic change.

Systemic Contributors to Homelessness

It's crucial to recognize that homelessness does not exist in isolation. It stems from a matrix of factors beyond individual control—economic downturns, lack of affordable housing, inadequate mental health services, and systemic inequality are just the tip of the iceberg. We will delve into how these elements collectively contribute to the crisis and why addressing them is vital for any long-term solution.

Policy Directions Rooted in Reality

Addressing homelessness effectively requires policies that tackle the root causes rather than merely managing symptoms. This section advocates for a shift in policy-making from short-term fixes to sustainable solutions. By focusing on comprehensive strategies such as housing-first approaches, increased support services, and economic reforms, we can create a foundation for lasting change.

Understanding homelessness through this broader lens enables us to redefine our approach and move towards more empathetic and practical solutions. It invites policymakers, community leaders, and citizens alike to reconsider their perceptions and engage in actions that address the real issues at hand.

This chapter is not just an academic discussion; it's a call to action—a plea for compassion intertwined with practical insights. Through exploring these themes, we aim to foster a deeper understanding of homelessness that transcends the simplistic blame on personal failure. Join us as we unpack these complexities and pave the way toward ending homelessness by 2035.

In the realm of homelessness, misconceptions and stigma abound, clouding our understanding of this complex issue. It is crucial to dispel these myths to pave the way for effective solutions. One prevalent misconception is that homelessness is solely a result of personal failure. This belief not only oversimplifies the root causes but also hinders the development of comprehensive strategies to address the problem. By attributing homelessness to individual shortcomings, we overlook the systemic issues at play, perpetuating a cycle of inadequate support and misguided policies.

Understanding homelessness as a consequence of broader

economic conditions and systemic failures is key to breaking free from this limiting narrative. It is not a matter of personal failure but rather a reflection of societal shortcomings and policy gaps. Factors such as lack of affordable housing, insufficient access to mental health services, and limited job opportunities all contribute to the pervasive issue of homelessness. By acknowledging these systemic issues, we can begin to unravel the complexities that underlie this crisis.

Challenging these misconceptions requires a shift in perspective, away from blaming individuals and towards addressing the structural inequalities that fuel homelessness. Only by recognizing the multifaceted nature of this issue can we hope to implement lasting solutions. The stigma associated with homelessness as a personal failure must be dismantled to make room for more compassionate and effective interventions.

As we delve deeper into the realities of homelessness, it becomes evident that personal failure is not the primary cause. Rather, it is a symptom of larger societal problems that have been overlooked for far too long. By reframing our understanding of homelessness, we open up new possibilities for meaningful change. It is not about pointing fingers at individuals but about **recognizing the collective responsibility** we have in creating a society where everyone has access to stable housing and supportive services.

Let's challenge these misconceptions together and uncover the truth behind homelessness.

This shift in mindset is crucial in our journey towards ending homelessness by 2035. By examining these myths and shedding light on the systemic issues at play, we can pave the way for transformative policies that address the root causes rather than just treating the symptoms. Join me as we explore further into the intricate web of factors contributing to homelessness and advocate for change that truly makes a difference in people's lives.

Systemic Issues Contributing to Homelessness

When we look at the issue of homelessness, it's crucial to recognize that it is not solely a result of personal failure or individual shortcomings. **Homelessness is often a symptom of systemic issues** that have been brewing beneath the surface for years. One of the key contributors to homelessness is the lack of affordable housing. As housing costs continue to rise, many individuals and families find themselves unable to keep up with rent payments, leading to eviction and ultimately, homelessness.

Another significant factor is the lack of a living wage. Many people working full-time jobs still struggle to make ends meet due to low wages that do not align with the rising cost of living. This disparity creates a cycle of poverty that can be incredibly challenging to break out of without adequate support systems in place.

Mental health issues and substance abuse also play a significant role in homelessness. Without proper access to mental health services or addiction treatment programs, individuals facing these challenges may find themselves on the streets with nowhere else to turn. It's essential to address these underlying issues with compassion and understanding rather than judgment and stigma.

The Intersectionality of Systemic Failures

Homelessness is not a singular issue; rather, it is an intersectional problem that stems from various systemic failures working in tandem. **Racial disparities in access to housing and employment opportunities** contribute significantly to the disproportionate number of people of color experiencing homelessness. Discriminatory practices in housing and hiring perpetuate cycles of poverty that are difficult to escape.

The criminal justice system also plays a role in perpetuating homelessness. Individuals with criminal records often face barriers to securing stable housing and employment, making it challenging for them to reintegrate into society after serving their time. This lack of support and reintegration resources can lead individuals down a path that ultimately leads to homelessness.

Breaking Down Barriers

To effectively address homelessness, we must first acknowledge and understand the systemic issues that contribute to this complex problem. By recognizing the intersectionality of factors such as affordable housing, living wages, mental health, substance abuse, racial disparities, and criminal justice involvement, we can begin to develop comprehensive solutions that address the root causes rather than just treating the symptoms.

Advocating for policies that promote affordable housing, fair wages, access to mental health services, addiction treatment programs, and reintegration support for formerly incarcerated individuals is essential in breaking down the barriers that keep people trapped in cycles of homelessness. By addressing these systemic issues head-on, we can create a more equitable society where everyone has access to stable housing and the support they need to thrive.

Advocating for Comprehensive Solutions

It is crucial to acknowledge that homelessness is not solely an individual issue but rather a symptom of larger systemic failures. To truly address the root causes of homelessness, we must advocate for policies that go beyond temporary fixes and tackle the underlying issues that perpetuate this crisis. **Merely addressing the symptoms without tackling the root causes is akin to putting a band-aid on a deep wound—it may provide temporary relief, but it does not heal the underlying problem.**

Embracing Compassionate Policies

Compassion should be at the heart of any policy aimed at ending homelessness. When crafting solutions, it is essential to consider the humanity and dignity of those experiencing homelessness. **Policies that prioritize empathy and understanding can lead to more effective and sustainable outcomes.** By approaching the issue with compassion, we can create policies that not only provide immediate support but also offer pathways to long-term stability and empowerment.

Shifting Focus to Prevention

Prevention is key in addressing homelessness. By implementing policies that focus on preventing individuals and families from becoming homeless in the first place, we can make significant strides in reducing the overall number of people experiencing homelessness. **Investing in affordable housing, mental health services, and job training programs can help prevent individuals from falling into homelessness due to economic hardships or personal crises.**

Collaborating Across Sectors

To effectively address homelessness, collaboration across sectors is essential. Policymakers, community organizations, businesses, and individuals all have a role to play in finding sustainable solutions to this complex issue. **By working together and leveraging each other's strengths, we can create comprehensive strategies that address the multifaceted nature of homelessness.**

Promoting Equity and Inclusion

It is crucial to center equity and inclusion in all efforts to end homelessness. **Recognizing the unique challenges faced by marginalized communities and ensuring that policies are inclusive and accessible to all is essential for creating lasting change.** By prioritizing equity, we can work towards a future where everyone has a safe place to call home.

Investing in Long-Term Solutions

Short-term solutions are important for immediate relief, but long-term investments are necessary for sustainable change. **By investing in affordable housing, mental health services, education, and job opportunities, we can create a foundation for individuals and families to build stable lives free from homelessness.** It is through these long-term investments that we can truly make a lasting impact on ending homelessness.

Empowering Communities to Drive Change

Communities play a vital role in addressing homelessness on a local level. **Empowering communities to take ownership of finding solutions tailored to their unique needs can lead to more effective outcomes.** By fostering collaboration and mobilizing resources within communities, we can create a network of support that helps individuals transition out of homelessness and into stable housing situations.

In advocating for policies that address the root causes of homelessness rather than just the symptoms, we pave the way for a more compassionate and effective approach to ending this crisis. It is through comprehensive strategies, collaborative efforts, and a commitment to equity that we can work towards a future where homelessness is no longer a pervasive issue in our society.

As we've traversed the terrain of homelessness, it's clear that the roots of this crisis extend far beyond personal mishaps or failures. The stigma that envelops those experiencing homelessness often blinds society to the systemic scaffolding that perpetuates this condition. By understanding homelessness through a lens that recognizes economic and systemic contributors, we open ourselves to solutions that are not only compassionate but also effective.

Homelessness is not a personal failure; rather, it's a complex issue entangled with economic downturns, lack of affordable housing, inadequate mental health services, and systemic barriers that prevent individuals from securing stable and affordable housing. Recognizing these factors shifts our approach from blame to support, from isolation to inclusion.

Advocating for policies that address these root causes is paramount. Instead of short-term fixes, we need robust, sustainable strategies—like increased funding for affordable housing, comprehensive mental health services, and employment programs that are accessible to all. These are not merely aids; they are investments in the future of our communities.

Imagine a society where policies reflect an understanding of these complexities, where systems are designed to lift individuals out of the cycle of homelessness rather than pushing them further into despair. This is not just a hopeful vision but a practical approach to dismantling the barriers that lead to homelessness.

Every step we take towards educating ourselves and advocating for informed policies reinforces the foundation for a society that upholds dignity and opportunity for all its members. Let us then move forward with a renewed commitment to not only understand but actively participate in resolving one of the most pressing issues of our times. Together, we can redefine the landscape of homelessness and transform lives for generations to come.

This chapter serves as a crucial pivot in our understanding of homelessness, steering us towards actions that address deeper societal issues rather than superficial symptoms. As we continue to explore the blueprint for ending homelessness by 2035, let's carry forward the insights gained here, applying them to forge pathways that lead to real change.

Chapter 3: The Economics of Inaction: Why We Can't Afford to Ignore Homelessness

In the dim light of early morning, Thomas sat at the worn kitchen table in his modest apartment, a cup of black coffee steaming beside him. The city was just beginning to stir outside his window, a soft symphony of distant traffic and the intermittent cry of a lone bird. He had been awake for hours, his mind wrestling with the numbers and reports scattered across the table.

Thomas worked as a policy advisor for the city council, and lately, his days, and many of his nights, had been consumed by one pressing issue: homelessness. The recent spike in the homeless population had reached an urgent peak, and with it came increased pressure on emergency services that were already stretched thin. He knew that something substantial needed to be done, but the sheer scale of financial investment required was daunting.

As he sipped his coffee, Thomas recalled a meeting from the previous week where he presented data to council members. He had tried to illustrate how investing in comprehensive housing-first programs could ultimately save money by reducing strain on emergency medical services, law enforcement involvement, and other social services. Yet despite his arguments and clear-cut data, skepticism was palpable; the upfront costs seemed to overshadow long-term savings in their minds.

The sound of his neighbor's door slamming pulled him back from his thoughts. He glanced out the window again, noticing a young woman across the street helping an older man settle onto a public bench with what looked like all his worldly possessions in a tattered backpack. The sight was all too common these days.

Turning back to his papers, Thomas began reworking his

presentation. He focused on refining how he communicated the economic sensibility behind strategic investments in resolving homelessness. It wasn't just about numbers; it was about real people whose lives could be dramatically improved with thoughtful policy changes.

As he aligned facts with empathetic narratives, highlighting stories like that of the old man on the bench, he hoped to paint a more compelling picture that could sway even the most fiscally conservative council member.

Would they see beyond immediate costs and recognize value in securing long-term social stability? Or would fiscal myopia continue to blind them from embracing solutions that not only resolved moral crises but also made economic sense?

The Hidden Price of Turning Away: Unveiling the True Cost of Homelessness

When faced with the stark realities of homelessness, it's tempting to think that looking away might save us money. Yet, **the truth tells a different story**. In the shadows of our cities, where the unfortunate roam without roofs, the cost of inaction not only weighs heavily on our moral compass but also on our economy. This chapter delves into a critical analysis, challenging the often short-sighted fiscal arguments against comprehensive homeless interventions.

At first glance, the dollars attached to initiatives aimed at eradicating homelessness can seem daunting. Policymakers and taxpayers alike may balk at the figures proposed for housing-first programs and comprehensive support services. However, when we peel back the layers, what becomes evident is that *the cost of ignoring this crisis far surpasses the investment required to solve it.* We will explore how emergency healthcare, law enforcement involvement, and ongoing social services for the homeless actually create a *greater financial burden* than preventative measures and stable housing solutions would.

The Economic Ripple Effects of Homelessness

Consider for a moment the frequent use of emergency rooms by homeless individuals as their primary healthcare provider. Not only is this an inefficient use of resources, but it's also one of the most expensive ways to deliver healthcare. Similarly, law enforcement officers spend countless hours addressing situations that are fundamentally social issues—not crimes—diverting resources from other critical community needs.

Moreover, homelessness exacerbates joblessness, which in turn fuels a cycle of poverty that impacts local economies. Businesses suffer from reduced consumer spending, neighborhoods bear the brunt of decreased property values, and cities lose out on potential revenue from otherwise productive individuals. This chapter will show how these costs accumulate over time, painting a clear picture that **doing nothing is far more expensive** than proactive intervention.

Investing Wisely: The Economic Case for Ending Homelessness

As we pivot to discussing investments in solutions for homelessness, we will outline how strategic funding can not only alleviate but also reverse these economic drains. Housing-first models have shown promising results where upfront investments lead to significant reductions in emergency service costs. By providing stable housing as a foundation, individuals are better positioned to utilize job training and education programs, contributing positively to their communities and local economies.

Furthermore, preventive services can drastically reduce the need for more costly interventions down the line. By ensuring access to mental health services and addiction treatment, among other supports, we can decrease the likelihood of repeated homelessness or prolonged reliance on emergency services.

Fiscal Prudence Requires Bold Action

The argument here is straightforward: investing in ending homelessness is not just compassionate; it is economically sensible. It aligns with principles of fiscal prudence by reducing long-term costs associated with managing its consequences. It's an investment in human potential, one that pays dividends in safer, healthier communities and stronger economies.

In this chapter, we will lay out a detailed comparison between the costs incurred through neglect versus those required for resolution. By examining data-driven research and real-world applications of successful programs, we'll make a compelling case for why now is the time to act, not just from a humanitarian perspective but from a financial one as well.

As we move forward in this discussion, remember: every dollar spent towards ending homelessness is not just a cost—it's an investment in our future. An investment that promises not only economic returns but also fosters a more inclusive and thriving society.

When we consider the costs associated with resolving homelessness versus the costs of inaction, a stark reality emerges. Initially, the idea of investing in Housing-First strategies and comprehensive support services may seem financially daunting. However, research consistently demonstrates that the price tag of homelessness on emergency medical services, law enforcement, and social services far surpasses the expenses involved in providing stable housing and preventive measures. The economic burden of allowing homelessness to persist unchecked is simply unsustainable.

Inaction comes at a high price. Emergency room visits, often utilized by individuals experiencing homelessness as their primary source of medical care, rack up substantial costs that are ultimately passed on to taxpayers. Law enforcement expenditures related to addressing issues stemming from homelessness, such as public disturbances or substance abuse problems, strain municipal budgets. Social services aimed at mitigating the effects of homelessness represent another significant financial drain. These cumulative expenses paint a clear picture: turning a blind eye to homelessness is not only morally unjust but also fiscally irresponsible.

On the other hand, investing in resolving homelessness makes economic sense. By providing stable housing and wraparound services through initiatives like Housing First, communities can address the root causes of homelessness and reduce reliance on costly emergency interventions. Studies have shown that when individuals are housed first, they are better able to address other challenges they may face, such as mental health issues or substance abuse. This approach leads to reduced strain on emergency services and paves the way for long-term cost savings.

The economics of homelessness demand a shift in perspective. Instead of viewing homelessness solely through a humanitarian lens, we must recognize it as an economic issue with far-reaching implications for society as a whole. By reframing our understanding of the problem, we can see that investing in solutions is not only the right thing to do ethically but also a wise financial decision in the long run.

Dive deeper into the financial implications of homelessness on emergency and social services.

Homelessness is not just a social issue; it has significant financial implications that extend to emergency and social services. The costs of homelessness on these services are substantial, often resulting in a drain on resources and taxpayer dollars. Emergency medical services are frequently utilized by individuals experiencing homelessness, as they lack access to preventative care and often seek medical attention only when their health concerns become severe. This leads to increased healthcare costs, as treating illnesses at advanced stages is more expensive than providing preventive care.

Law enforcement agencies also bear a considerable burden due to homelessness. Individuals without stable housing are more likely to be involved in interactions with law enforcement, whether due to loitering, petty crimes, or other issues associated with their living situation. This places strain on police resources and the criminal justice system, diverting attention from other pressing matters in the community. Moreover, the revolving door of arrests and incarcerations for individuals experiencing homelessness contributes to a cycle of poverty and legal entanglements that is costly for society as a whole.

Social services are also heavily impacted by homelessness, as agencies work tirelessly to provide support and resources to those in need. However, the demand often outweighs the available resources, leading to overextended services and burnout among social workers. Additionally, the lack of stable housing exacerbates existing social issues such as mental health challenges, substance abuse, and family instability, requiring more intensive interventions that strain the social services system.

The financial toll of homelessness on emergency and social services is undeniable.

Addressing homelessness at its root cause by providing stable housing solutions not only benefits individuals but also alleviates the strain on emergency and social services. By ensuring that individuals have access to safe and stable housing, we can reduce their reliance on emergency medical services, thus lowering healthcare costs in the long run. Furthermore, stable housing decreases interactions with law enforcement, leading to a reduction in associated costs and allowing police resources to be allocated more effectively within communities.

Investing in homelessness resolution is not just a moral imperative; it is an economic necessity.

Preventative measures such as Housing-First strategies have been proven to be cost-effective in the long term by reducing the strain on emergency and social services caused by homelessness. By investing in solutions that address the root causes of homelessness, we can create a more sustainable system that benefits both individuals and society as a whole. **The economic argument for resolving homelessness is clear: the cost of inaction far outweighs the cost of implementing effective solutions.**

Investing in resolving homelessness is not just a compassionate act; it also makes economic sense. By shifting our focus from managing the consequences of homelessness to preventing it, we can save significant resources in the long run. **Providing stable housing and support services may seem like a costly endeavor upfront, but the financial benefits outweigh the initial investment.** Research consistently shows that the expenses incurred from emergency medical services, law enforcement, and social services due to homelessness far surpass the costs of implementing Housing-First strategies and other preventive measures.

The economic argument for addressing homelessness is compelling. When individuals have access to stable housing, they are less likely to rely on costly emergency services for their basic needs. By providing supportive services along with housing, we can address the root causes of homelessness and reduce the strain on public resources. This proactive approach not only improves the quality of life for those experiencing homelessness but also leads to cost savings across various sectors.

Preventive measures are key to long-term economic stability. Investing in programs that address homelessness at its core can break the cycle of poverty and reduce reliance on public assistance programs. When individuals have a stable foundation, they are more likely to secure employment, contribute to the economy, and become self-sufficient. This ripple effect benefits not only those directly impacted by homelessness but society as a whole.

Furthermore, failing to address homelessness has far-reaching economic consequences. The costs associated with emergency room visits, incarceration, and other crisis interventions add up quickly. These reactive measures drain resources without addressing the underlying issue, perpetuating a cycle of dependence on expensive public services. By contrast, investing in homelessness resolution is an investment in long-term savings and sustainable community development.

It's essential to consider the broader economic impact of homelessness on society as a whole. When individuals lack stable housing, it affects not only their well-being but also the overall health of communities. Homelessness can lead to increased crime rates, decreased property values, and strained social services. By investing in solutions that address homelessness comprehensively, we can create healthier, more resilient communities for everyone.

In conclusion, prioritizing investments in resolving homelessness is not just a moral imperative; it is a strategic economic decision. By redirecting resources towards preventive measures and supportive services, we can create a more efficient and sustainable system that benefits individuals, communities, and society as a whole. Through thoughtful planning and strategic investments, we can work towards ending homelessness by 2035 and building a brighter future for all.

The stark reality that emerges from our discussion is simple: the cost of ignoring homelessness far surpasses the expenses involved in solving it. It's much like watching a leak worsen in the ceiling of your home—initially, the damage might seem manageable, but over time, the costs of repair can skyrocket as the structure becomes more compromised.

In assessing the financial toll on emergency and social services, we see a clear pattern: **public systems are strained** by the high demands of homelessness. Emergency rooms, law enforcement, and social service agencies bear the brunt, spending vast resources on acute care rather than preventive measures. This is not just a drain on rcsources but a less effective way of managing public funds.

From an economic standpoint, investing in comprehensive solutions to homelessness is not merely a moral obligation but a financially sound strategy. Consider it an upfront investment in community health and safety that yields significant returns over time. By shifting our focus from intermittent care to stable housing solutions, we not only alleviate the immediate pressures on public services but also foster a more sustainable economic environment.

This approach does not suggest a mere increase in spending but rather a strategic redirection of funds. It's akin to opting for a sturdy, well-made pair of boots that will last for years over cheaper, less durable options that need frequent replacement. The initial cost is higher, but the long-term savings are undeniable.

As we move forward into subsequent discussions, let us keep in mind that the economics of resolving homelessness are compelling. They beckon us not just to act but to act wisely, harnessing our collective resources to build a foundation where every individual has the stability necessary to contribute to and thrive in our society.

Thus, as we consider our strategies and policies, let's view them through the lens of economic sensibility and long-term community benefit. The path is clear; the rationale for action is sound. Let us step forward with the knowledge that our efforts are not just acts of compassion but pragmatic steps towards a stronger, more resilient society.

Chapter 4:
Housing First: A Foundation for Stability

In the cool shade of an early spring morning, Thomas sat on the worn wooden steps of his front porch, a notebook rested loosely in his lap. He watched as the neighborhood stirred to life; children chased each other with the careless abandon only seen in those who have not yet felt the weight of the world. His thoughts wandered to his own childhood, fleeting images of laughter and warmth that now seemed distant as he faced a problem that gnawed at him with increasing urgency.

The city council had recently approved a new initiative aimed at tackling homelessness—a subject close to Thomas's heart since his brother had spent years on the streets, caught in a cycle of temporary solutions and conditional housing offers. The new policy was centered around a Housing-First model, which provided housing without preconditions like sobriety or employment. Thomas mulled over this approach, wondering if it might have changed his brother's fate.

As he scribbled down notes, an elderly neighbor passed by, her steps slow but determined. She nodded at Thomas with a gentle smile that spoke volumes of her enduring spirit despite years of witnessing the neighborhood's struggles.

"Morning, Mrs. Elkins," Thomas called out softly.

"Good morning, dear," she replied. "Working on your big project?"

"Yes," he said, pausing to look up from his notebook. "Trying to figure out how unconditional housing could actually work here."

Mrs. Elkins stopped and considered this for a moment. "You know," she began thoughtfully, "everyone deserves a place to call home without strings attached."

Her words echoed in his mind as Thomas turned back to his notes. The effectiveness of unconditional housing strategies was clear in theory—providing stability and safety first could indeed be the cornerstone for addressing more complex personal issues later on. Yet how would it play out here? How would it change lives?

The sun climbed higher in the sky, casting long shadows across his pages filled with doubts and possibilities alike. A dog barked somewhere in the distance; its sound was sharp against the soft rustling leaves above him.

By afternoon, Thomas had outlined several key points: stable housing as a critical first step towards solving homelessness seemed logical yet radical given traditional models that demanded proof of 'worthiness' before assistance was granted. He knew there would be pushback from various quarters—fiscal conservatives worried about costs; residents concerned about property values; skeptics questioning long-term outcomes.

But then there were people like Mrs. Elkins—those who understood human dignity did not come preconditioned.

As dusk painted the sky with strokes of pink and orange, Thomas remained seated on those steps, feeling both overwhelmed and hopeful. This issue was personal; it touched something deep within him—a desire for justice and compassion that went beyond mere policy changes or statistical victories.

He closed his notebook slowly as another neighbor walked by with their child pointing excitedly at a budding tree along their path—an emblem of new beginnings.

Could this community embrace such a transformative idea? Could they see beyond conditions to possibilities?

From Houses to Homes: Rethinking the Path to Stability

When we consider the myriad issues plaguing society today, homelessness stands out as both urgent and heartbreakingly visible.

The traditional approach to resolving homelessness often hinges on conditional models, where housing is a reward for meeting certain criteria like sobriety or employment. However, emerging evidence suggests that these methods might not only be ineffective but could actually exacerbate the problem. This chapter delves into the transformative potential of **Housing First**, a strategy that prioritizes providing the homeless with housing without preconditions, thereby offering a stable foundation from which individuals can address other personal challenges.

The Paradigm Shift in Homeless Assistance

The shift from conditional to unconditional housing models marks a significant evolution in how we address homelessness. *Housing First* isn't just about placing roofs over heads; it's about affirming dignity and fostering long-term stability. This approach challenges the conventional wisdom that people must earn their right to housing by first overcoming personal challenges. Instead, it posits that the security of a home is the best foundation upon which individuals can begin to tackle these issues, be they related to health, addiction, or unemployment.

Examining Effectiveness

In evaluating the effectiveness of unconditional housing strategies, we will explore data and case studies that illuminate how these approaches have fared across different regions and communities. Studies consistently show that when people are provided with stable housing without preconditions, they are more likely to remain housed and less likely to fall back into homelessness. This is more than an ideological shift; it's a pragmatic strategy backed by compelling evidence of success.

Why Stability Matters

At its core, stable housing is more than just a shelter—it's a platform for life. Without the constant anxiety of where one will sleep each night or whether they will find shelter from the elements, individuals are better positioned to seek employment, maintain health treatments, and engage with community services. The importance of this stability cannot be overstated; it is often the first critical step toward sustainable personal development and societal integration.

The conversation around Housing First also intersects with broader social issues, including healthcare access, mental health support, and economic inequality. By unconditionally providing homes to those in need, not only are we addressing the surface issue of homelessness but also beginning to untangle some of the deeper societal knots that contribute to this condition.

Moving Forward

As we delve deeper into this discussion in subsequent sections, keep in mind the transformative power of viewing a house not just as four walls and a roof but as a home, a fundamental human right that provides security, warmth, and dignity. By rethinking our approach to helping those without homes, we are not merely offering them shelter but are actively participating in reshaping their future—and ours.

Through this chapter's exploration of Housing First models contrasted with conditional approaches, our aim is not just to critique but to illuminate paths forward that could fundamentally alter how society deals with one of its most persistent challenges. Let us consider how unconditional housing can serve as both a moral imperative and a practical solution in our shared quest to end homelessness by 2035.

Housing strategies for the homeless vary widely, but one stark division exists between conditional housing approaches and Housing First models. **Conditional housing programs** typically require individuals to meet certain criteria before they can access stable housing. These conditions might include maintaining sobriety, engaging in specific treatment programs, or securing employment. While these conditions are often well-intentioned, they can create significant barriers for individuals experiencing homelessness.

In contrast, **Housing First** models prioritize providing immediate access to stable housing without imposing preconditions. This approach recognizes that secure housing is a fundamental human need and a critical first step in addressing other challenges faced by individuals experiencing homelessness. By removing barriers to housing, such as the need to be sober or employed, Housing First models offer a more inclusive and effective solution for those in need.

Conditional housing approaches can unintentionally perpetuate cycles of homelessness by making it challenging for individuals to secure stable housing. Requiring individuals to meet specific criteria before accessing housing can prolong their experience of homelessness and exacerbate existing issues. In contrast, Housing First models acknowledge that stability in housing is essential for individuals to address other challenges they may be facing, such as substance abuse or mental health issues.

One key difference between conditional housing and Housing First models lies in their underlying philosophies. **Conditional housing** operates on the premise that individuals must demonstrate readiness or compliance with certain expectations before receiving assistance. On the other hand, **Housing First** recognizes that stable housing is a basic human right and provides a foundation from which individuals can address other aspects of their lives.

By prioritizing immediate access to stable housing, Housing First models have demonstrated higher success rates in helping individuals maintain long-term housing stability. This approach has proven particularly effective for individuals with complex needs who may struggle to meet the requirements of traditional conditional housing programs. Providing unconditional support through Housing First allows individuals to focus on stabilizing their lives without the added stress of meeting predetermined conditions.

Continue reading to explore the effectiveness of unconditional housing strategies and their impact on long-term stability for the homeless community.

Unconditional housing strategies have proven to be significantly more effective in addressing homelessness than conditional approaches. By providing stable housing without preconditions such as sobriety or employment, individuals experiencing homelessness are better able to focus on their overall well-being and address the root causes of their housing instability. **This approach recognizes that secure housing is a fundamental human need** and provides a solid foundation upon which individuals can rebuild their lives.

Research has shown that unconditional housing leads to higher success rates in maintaining long-term housing stability. When individuals are not burdened by the pressure of meeting certain conditions, they can access the support services they need to address underlying issues such as mental health challenges, substance abuse, or lack of education. **Unconditional housing allows individuals to prioritize their health and well-being**, leading to better outcomes in terms of housing retention and overall quality of life.

By removing barriers to housing, unconditional strategies pave the way for individuals experiencing homelessness to access the resources and support they need. When individuals have a stable place to call home, they are more likely to engage with case managers, healthcare providers, and social services, leading to improved outcomes in areas such as employment, education, and mental health. **Unconditional housing creates a sense of security and stability that empowers individuals to make positive changes in their lives**.

Conditional approaches, on the other hand, often create additional obstacles for individuals experiencing homelessness.

Requiring sobriety or employment as prerequisites for housing can perpetuate cycles of homelessness by making it harder for individuals to access the support they need. **These conditions can be especially challenging for individuals dealing with complex issues such as addiction or mental illness**, further marginalizing those who are already vulnerable.

In contrast, unconditional housing models embrace a compassionate and holistic approach to addressing homelessness. By recognizing that stable housing is a basic human right, these models prioritize dignity and respect for individuals experiencing homelessness. **Unconditional housing sends a powerful message that everyone deserves a safe place to live**, regardless of their past experiences or current circumstances.

Ultimately, unconditional housing strategies offer a more humane and effective solution to homelessness. By focusing on providing stable housing first and foremost, these models set individuals up for long-term success by addressing their immediate needs and creating a pathway to self-sufficiency. **By investing in unconditional housing, communities can make significant strides towards ending homelessness and creating a more equitable society for all**.

Housing First Process Model

In the Housing First process model, the initial step involves **identifying homeless individuals** and **assessing their needs**. This critical phase highlights the importance of understanding the unique circumstances of each person without imposing preconditions for housing. By focusing on individual needs rather than blanket requirements like sobriety or employment, the model ensures a personalized approach to addressing homelessness.

The next stage in the model revolves around **providing immediate access to permanent housing**. This key element sets Housing First apart from traditional approaches by prioritizing stable accommodation as the first step towards stability. By offering a secure place to live without prerequisites, individuals can begin to rebuild their lives with a sense of security and dignity.

Following secure housing, the model incorporates **wrap-around support services** tailored to individual requirements. These services may include job training, addiction treatment, mental health care, and other essential supports. By offering a comprehensive range of assistance, Housing First addresses the root causes of homelessness while empowering individuals to make sustainable changes in their lives.

The Housing First model emphasizes a **non-linear, client-driven approach**, recognizing that progress is not always a straightforward path. This flexibility allows for adjustments based on individual needs and preferences, fostering a sense of autonomy and empowerment among those experiencing homelessness.

Central to the model are **key decision points** that guide service provision and support adaptation. These decision points ensure that interventions remain responsive to changing circumstances, promoting long-term success in maintaining housing stability.

Moreover, the inclusion of **feedback loops** underscores the iterative nature of the process. By collecting feedback from residents and evaluating outcomes, service providers can refine their strategies to better meet the evolving needs of those they serve.

External factors such as **funding sources**, **community support**, and **regulatory environments** also play a crucial role in shaping each stage of the model. These influences highlight the interconnected nature of addressing homelessness and underscore the importance of collaboration across various sectors.

By showcasing successful case studies of Housing First implementations, stakeholders can gain practical insights into effective strategies and outcomes. These real-world examples offer tangible evidence of the model's effectiveness and provide inspiration for communities seeking to implement similar approaches.

The Housing First process model offers a clear, actionable framework for addressing homelessness by prioritizing stable housing as a critical first step towards long-term stability. Through its client-centered approach, comprehensive support services, and emphasis on flexibility and feedback, this model provides a roadmap for communities to create lasting change for individuals experiencing homelessness.

The Pathway to Stability: A Step-by-Step Guide to Transformative Housing Solutions

In the realm of addressing homelessness, the contrast between Housing First models and conditional housing approaches reveals a significant shift in strategy. Housing First, by providing immediate access to permanent housing coupled with individualized support services, has consistently been shown to foster long-term stability. This chapter has unpacked these models, demonstrating their superiority over traditional conditional approaches that require individuals to meet specific prerequisites like sobriety or employment before offering assistance.

The initial step in our exploration was understanding the core concepts of Housing First. We've seen that this model isn't merely about handing over keys but about nurturing an environment where the formerly homeless can thrive. Evidence points to its success in not only maintaining housing stability but also in improving overall well-being.

Moving forward, **we contrasted** this with conditional housing approaches, which often erect barriers that can exacerbate the challenges faced by those in need. By requiring individuals to qualify for housing through various preconditions, these models potentially delay or deny access to the very resource that is foundational to personal stability.

Our evaluation of unconditional housing strategies brought to light their profound impact. Studies and firsthand accounts have illustrated how unconditional access to housing leads to improved health outcomes, a decrease in homelessness recurrence, and overall cost-effectiveness. This evidence robustly counters criticisms that might undervalue the practicality of Housing First approaches.

Finally, we recognized **the critical importance of stable housing** as more than a mere shelter. It is the cornerstone upon which individuals rebuild their lives—addressing health issues, seeking employment, and restoring relationships. Success stories abound, showcasing real people whose lives have been transformed through the stability provided by Housing First models.

This journey through Housing First models highlights their role not just in combating homelessness but in fostering a society where every individual has the opportunity to recover and thrive. As we move forward, it is imperative that policymakers and community leaders continue to advocate for and implement these proven strategies. By doing so, we uphold the belief that access to stable housing is not only a basic human right but a critical societal investment.

By embracing these insights and pushing for broader adoption, we inch closer to a future where homelessness is not an insurmountable issue but a challenge met with effective, compassionate responses. Let us carry forward the lessons learned here and integrate them into our ongoing efforts to ensure that no individual is without a place to call home.

Chapter 5: Economic Safety Nets: Preventing Homelessness Through Job Security

Late afternoon sunlight filtered through the high windows of the community center, casting long shadows on the worn linoleum floor. George, a middle-aged man with deep-set eyes and a persistent furrow in his brow, sat at one of the round tables scattered around the room. His fingers tapped a steady rhythm on the tabletop, echoing his thoughts that raced as fast as his heart in moments of worry. He was here for a meeting about economic policies aimed at preventing homelessness, a cause not just close to his heart but woven into his very being.

Years ago, George had faced nights under the cold bridge of Fourth Street with nothing but a threadbare jacket and a haunting hunger for company. Those memories clung to him like the chill of those nights, never quite leaving his bones no matter how far he'd come. Now housed and steady, he couldn't shake off the dread that it could all unravel again without solid ground beneath anyone's feet.

Across from him sat Emily, a young woman with sharp eyes and an earnestness that made her appear older than her years. She was speaking passionately about job training programs and how they were essential in giving people not just skills but also dignity—something George knew all too well was first to be stripped away by hardship. "When people can stand on their own two feet, earn fair wages, they're not just working; they're building lives," she said.

The room hummed with murmurs of agreement and cups clinking against saucers as volunteers passed around refreshments. The scent of coffee mingled with baked goods filled the air, grounding George's swirling thoughts. He noticed an older woman nodding vigorously at Emily's words, her hands trembling slightly as she lifted her cup.

A child's laughter broke through the serious tones of discussion when a little girl darted between tables, playing tag with her shadow. It reminded George of what was at stake, the future generations who deserved better than fear and uncertainty about their homes and meals.

As he listened to proposals for accessible quality education as another pillar to prevent homelessness, George's mind traced back to his own days of trying to study in public libraries, clinging onto every word read under dim table lamps as if they were lifelines thrown into turbulent seas.

The meeting drew to a close with promises of action and commitments renewed. People began drifting towards the door in twos and threes, their voices low but determined. George stayed seated for a moment longer; he felt anchored there by both weighty memories and blossoming hope.

As he finally stood up to leave, catching sight of his reflection in one of the glass-paneled doors, a reflection now filled out and far removed from those frail days under bridges, he wondered if these policies could indeed weave safety nets tight enough so no one would slip through again like he once did.

Could economic stability really ensure no child would have to play tag alone in shadows cast by uncertainty?

Unraveling the Threads of Economic Security to Weave a Stronger Safety Net

Economic stability forms the bedrock upon which individuals build their lives, yet for many, this foundation is fraught with instability and uncertainty. In a country as affluent as America, the persistence of homelessness challenges the very ethos of opportunity and equality we cherish. This chapter delves into the significant role economic policies play in preventing homelessness by fostering job security, advocating for fair wage practices, and underscoring the importance of accessible quality education.

The Pillars of Prevention: Economic Policies and Homelessness

At the heart of preventing homelessness lies a critical need for robust economic policies that not only address immediate needs but also forestall future crises. It is essential to understand that homelessness is often a symptom of larger economic vulnerabilities; it's not merely about the lack of housing but about the absence of sustainable economic opportunities. By implementing policies aimed at enhancing job security and ensuring fair wages, we can provide a more predictable environment for at-risk populations.

Equipping for Tomorrow: The Role of Job Training

Job training programs stand as crucial bridges connecting individuals with the skills necessary to participate effectively in an evolving workforce. These programs do more than teach skills; they empower individuals, giving them the tools to navigate and adapt to complex job markets. Highlighting successful models of job training initiatives will showcase how targeted educational resources can significantly alter the trajectory from potential homelessness to stable employment.

A Fair Wage: The Foundation of Economic Stability

Discussing fair wage policies is not just about numbers on a paycheck; it's about ensuring dignity and sustainability in employment. A fair minimum wage can dramatically impact the ability to secure stable housing by providing workers with enough income not only to survive but also to plan and save for the future. By advocating for wages that reflect living costs, we take a vital step towards diminishing the risk of homelessness.

Education: Unlocking Doors to Stability

Accessible quality education acts as a cornerstone in preventing homelessness by equipping individuals with critical thinking skills, knowledge, and qualifications needed in today’s job market.

Exploring how education systems can be made more inclusive will help us understand its direct impact on reducing vulnerabilities that lead to homelessness.

This chapter will explore these themes in depth, aiming not only to present facts but also to engage with ideas that challenge our understanding and compel us to action. Through a careful examination of economic policies, job training programs, fair wage laws, and educational accessibility, we can create more than just safety nets; we can build trampolines that propel individuals towards stability and success.

By addressing these foundational elements, we are not merely patching up holes but are actively constructing a framework that supports all citizens, ensuring that economic insecurity no longer leads to homelessness. Engaging with these points allows us not only to envision a future where homelessness is rare but also to take deliberate steps towards realizing this vision. This approach does not simply manage the symptoms but addresses the root causes, paving the way towards enduring solutions in our quest to end homelessness by 2035.

Economic policies play a crucial role in preventing homelessness. By addressing the root causes of economic insecurity, we can create a safety net that helps individuals and families stay housed. Job security is a key component of this safety net, ensuring that people have stable employment and income to afford housing. When economic policies prioritize job security, they contribute significantly to reducing homelessness rates.

One of the primary ways to prevent homelessness is by implementing better job training programs. These programs equip individuals with the skills they need to secure stable employment and advance in their careers. By investing in job training initiatives, we can empower people to access higher-paying jobs that provide financial stability. This not only benefits individuals by increasing their earning potential but also strengthens the overall economy by creating a skilled workforce.

Accessible quality education is another essential aspect of economic policies that prevent homelessness. Education opens doors to better job opportunities and higher incomes, reducing the risk of housing instability. By ensuring that education is affordable and accessible to all, we can level the playing field and give everyone an equal chance at economic success. Quality education equips individuals with the knowledge and skills needed to thrive in today's competitive job market.

Fair minimum wage laws are also critical in preventing homelessness. When workers are paid a fair wage for their labor, they are better able to afford housing and meet their basic needs. A living wage ensures that individuals can support themselves and their families without having to choose between paying rent and putting food on the table. By enacting fair minimum wage laws, we can uplift low-income workers and reduce the risk of homelessness among vulnerable populations.

Let's delve deeper into how job training programs and fair wage policies can make a significant impact in preventing homelessness.

Advocate for job training and fair wage policies

One of the most effective ways to prevent homelessness is by advocating for job training programs and fair wage policies. **Job training programs** play a crucial role in equipping individuals with the skills and knowledge needed to secure stable employment. By investing in these programs, we can empower people to access better job opportunities, ultimately reducing the risk of economic instability that can lead to homelessness.

Fair wage policies are equally essential in ensuring that individuals can earn a livable income. When workers are paid fairly for their labor, they are better able to meet their basic needs, such as housing, food, and healthcare. Fair wages provide a sense of financial security that is vital in preventing homelessness among vulnerable populations.

By advocating for job training and fair wage policies, we are not only addressing the immediate needs of individuals but also creating long-term solutions to combat homelessness. When people have access to quality training and fair wages, they are more likely to achieve financial stability and independence, reducing their reliance on emergency services and public assistance programs.

Investing in job training programs is an investment in the future of our communities. By providing individuals with the opportunity to learn new skills and pursue fulfilling careers, we are not only empowering them but also strengthening our economy as a whole. When people are gainfully employed and earn fair livable wages, they contribute to the growth and prosperity of their communities.

Fair wage policies are a cornerstone of a just society. When workers are paid fairly, they are more likely to experience overall well-being and security. Fair wages ensure that individuals can afford safe and stable housing, access healthcare when needed, and provide for their families without constantly living on the brink of financial crisis.

Advocating for job training programs and fair wage policies is not just about economic stability; it is about upholding the dignity and worth of every individual. When we support initiatives that promote job security and fair compensation, we are sending a powerful message that everyone deserves the opportunity to thrive and succeed.

In conclusion, by prioritizing job training and fair wage policies, we can create a more equitable society where everyone has the chance to build a better future for themselves and their families. Let us continue to advocate for these essential initiatives as part of our comprehensive approach to ending homelessness by 2035.

Accessible quality education plays a crucial role in preventing homelessness by equipping individuals with the skills and knowledge needed to secure stable employment and financial stability. **Education is not just about acquiring knowledge; it is a powerful tool that can break the cycle of poverty and homelessness**. By providing individuals with quality education, we empower them to pursue better job opportunities, increase their earning potential, and ultimately improve their overall quality of life.

Investing in education is investing in the future. When individuals have access to quality education, they are better equipped to navigate the complexities of the job market and adapt to changing economic landscapes. Quality education goes beyond basic literacy and numeracy; it encompasses critical thinking skills, problem-solving abilities, and the capacity to learn new skills throughout one's lifetime. **Education is a pathway to empowerment**.

Quality education fosters resilience. It provides individuals with the tools to overcome challenges, adapt to setbacks, and pursue new opportunities. By instilling a sense of confidence and self-reliance, education enables individuals to weather economic storms and navigate through difficult times without falling into homelessness. **It acts as a safety net, offering stability and security even in the face of adversity**.

Accessible education is essential for all individuals, regardless of their background or circumstances. By ensuring that education is affordable, inclusive, and tailored to meet diverse needs, we can level the playing field and provide equal opportunities for all. **Education should not be a privilege but a fundamental right** that empowers individuals to build a better future for themselves and their communities.

Education empowers individuals to make informed decisions about their career paths. By offering guidance, mentorship, and practical skills training, educational institutions can help individuals identify their strengths, interests, and goals. This guidance is essential in steering individuals away from precarious employment situations that could potentially lead to homelessness.

Investing in education is an investment in social mobility. By providing individuals with the tools they need to succeed in the workforce, we can create a more equitable society where everyone has the opportunity to thrive. Quality education breaks down barriers, opens doors to new possibilities, and paves the way for a brighter future for all.

In conclusion, accessible quality education is a powerful weapon against homelessness. **By empowering individuals with knowledge, skills, and opportunities**, we can prevent homelessness at its root cause - economic insecurity. Education not only transforms lives but also builds stronger communities where everyone has the chance to succeed.

Blueprint for Stability: A Three-Step Strategy

We've journeyed through the intricate relationship between economic stability and homelessness, uncovering how vital robust economic policies are to preventing this social issue. At the heart of our discussion is the undeniable truth that **economic insecurity needs to be targeted** to prevent homelessness effectively.

Step 1: Linking Economic Policy and Housing Stability

The first step in our blueprint focuses on the **critical role of economic policies** in maintaining housing stability. By understanding that unemployment, underemployment, and insufficient wages directly contribute to housing instability, we can advocate for policies that prioritize job security and fair wages. These policies are not just lines on paper; they are lifelines for millions at risk of homelessness.

Step 2: The Role of Job Training and Fair Wages

Next, we delve into the transformative potential of **job training and fair wage policies**. Skills development programs are more than educational benefits; they are a bridge to sustainable employment and a safeguard against the economic vulnerability that can lead to homelessness. By highlighting successful initiatives, we see firsthand how equipping individuals with the necessary skills fosters long-term employment and financial stability. Fair wage policies complement this by ensuring that work leads to genuine economic upliftment, breaking the cycle of poverty that often drives homelessness.

Step 3: Empowering Through Education

Our final step explores the powerful impact of **accessible, quality education** on preventing homelessness. Education is not merely about acquiring knowledge; it's about empowering individuals with the tools to build stable, secure lives. By making education accessible and relevant, we equip people with the armor to combat economic challenges effectively, thereby preventing homelessness. Successful educational initiatives demonstrate that when people can access the right resources, they can escape the traps of poverty and instability.

This three-step strategy isn't just a plan; it's a commitment to change, a series of actionable steps that, if followed diligently, can significantly reduce homelessness in America by targeting one of its root causes: economic insecurity. Each step is designed to build on the previous one, creating a comprehensive approach to tackling this pressing issue.

By embracing these strategies, communities and policymakers can work together to construct a safety net so robust that homelessness becomes a rare exception rather than a common fear. This is our blueprint for stability—a guide that if followed, promises not just to reduce homelessness but to transform lives.

Chapter 6: Building Solutions: Making Affordable Housing Accessible

In the early hours of a crisp autumn morning, Thomas walked through the bustling city streets lined with towering buildings that seemed to touch the sky. He passed by people of all walks, each absorbed in their own routines, seemingly oblivious to the world around them. The air was filled with the scent of rain from the night before, mingling with the exhaust from cars. Thomas's breath formed small clouds as he exhaled, his hands buried deep in his coat pockets.

Thomas was a city planner, deeply entrenched in the ongoing struggle against homelessness—a battle waged not just on cold streets but within paneled conference rooms and between lines of legislative text. Today, he was on his way to a critical meeting where he hoped to advocate for substantial changes in zoning laws and housing policies.

As he walked, his mind raced over past meetings: faces of opposition and support, arguments made with passion or cold indifference. He remembered one young woman's story vividly, a single mother displaced due to rising rents, her plight had stayed with him, fueling his resolve.

At a street corner, while waiting for the light to change, Thomas watched a small group huddled under an awning—a temporary shelter from life's harshness. Their eyes briefly met his; there was resignation in their gaze that struck him every time. It wasn't just about numbers and policies; it was about these human moments.

He crossed when the light turned green and entered a coffee shop bustling with early morning activity. The sound of milk steaming and orders being called out did little to distract him from his thoughts. As he waited for his tea at a corner table, he scribbled notes onto a napkin, ideas sparked by urgency: incentives for non-profit housing developers and more aggressive rental subsidies.

His phone vibrated with an email notification, an update from a colleague sharing preliminary data on how new zoning proposals could increase affordable housing units significantly if passed. This data could be pivotal today; it provided concrete evidence that change was possible—and necessary.

Thomas left the shop feeling fortified not by the tea but by renewed conviction. As he approached city hall, where decisions were made that shaped thousands of lives daily, he felt both its weight and potential.

Could they see beyond the bureaucracy today? Could they grasp that every policy shaped real lives—lives like those huddled under awnings or those forced into impossible choices between rent and food? Could today be different?

As Thomas pushed open the heavy doors to enter city hall's chambers armed with data and determination, one question lingered: Would they finally listen?

Is Affordable Housing the Keystone to Ending Homelessness?

The stark reality of homelessness in America is both visible and alarming, yet beneath the surface complexities lies a beacon of hope: affordable housing. As we navigate through the intricate landscape of social policies and economic strategies in our quest to end homelessness by 2035, it becomes increasingly clear that **affordable housing is not just a component but a cornerstone** of the solution. This chapter delves into the critical need for expanding affordable housing as a direct response to homelessness, exploring transformative policies and innovative community-driven solutions.

The Scarcity Crisis

At the heart of the homelessness issue is a glaring scarcity of affordable housing. It's a straightforward equation: without enough affordable homes, more people are at risk of homelessness. But why is there such a shortage? The reasons are manifold, involving economic, regulatory, and social factors. This chapter will outline these complexities not merely to describe a problem but to set the stage for actionable solutions.

Policy Levers for Change

Policy changes are pivotal in crafting a future where everyone has access to affordable housing. Zoning laws currently act as gatekeepers in many cities, deciding who gets to live where and at what cost. By advocating for reform in these laws, we can open up new opportunities for housing development that meets the needs of lower-income families. Additionally, rental subsidies play an essential role by bridging the gap between what residents can afford and the market rates. This chapter will illustrate how these policy tools can be reimagined and effectively implemented to create significant impacts.

Empowering Non-Profit Developers

Non-profit housing developers are often on the front lines of the affordable housing crisis, yet they face numerous obstacles, from funding shortages to bureaucratic red tape. Supporting these organizations is not just about providing financial resources; it's about creating an environment where they can succeed and expand their operations. This chapter will explore how public policies and community support can enhance the capabilities of non-profits, turning them into powerful engines for change in the housing sector.

Through detailed analysis and engaging discussion, this introduction sets up a comprehensive exploration of how targeted actions can address one of America's most pressing issues, homelessness. By understanding the pivotal role of affordable housing and rallying support for key policy reforms and initiatives, we can build a foundation for lasting change.

In navigating these discussions, we adopt a perspective that sees potential where others see despair, a perspective that seeks not only to inform but also to inspire action. The journey towards ending homelessness is undoubtedly complex, involving myriad stakeholders and requiring sustained commitment. Yet, with each step forward in addressing the affordable housing shortage through thoughtful policies and robust community engagement, we move closer to realizing that vision.

This chapter aims not just to present facts but to engage you in a dialogue about possibilities, about how each one of us can play a role in shaping a future where no American is homeless due to a lack of affordable housing. Let's explore together how we can turn this blueprint into reality.

Addressing the scarcity of affordable housing is crucial in the fight against homelessness. The lack of affordable housing options is a significant barrier that prevents individuals and families from securing stable and safe shelter. Without accessible housing that fits within their financial means, many find themselves at risk of homelessness or trapped in cycles of poverty. It is essential to recognize that homelessness cannot be effectively addressed without first tackling the root issue of affordable housing availability.

Affordable housing is not just a matter of convenience; it is a fundamental human right. Everyone deserves a place to call home, a place where they can feel secure, build a future, and contribute to their community. When individuals are forced to choose between paying for basic necessities like food and healthcare or their rent, it creates a cycle of instability that can lead to homelessness. By addressing the scarcity of affordable housing, we can break this cycle and provide individuals with the stability they need to thrive.

The shortage of affordable housing is a complex issue that requires multifaceted solutions. From rising rental costs to limited housing stock, various factors contribute to the affordability crisis. Addressing these challenges requires a comprehensive approach that involves policymakers, community leaders, developers, and advocates working together to create sustainable solutions. It is not enough to simply acknowledge the problem; action must be taken to implement tangible changes that will make affordable housing more accessible for all.

Investing in affordable housing is an investment in our communities. When individuals have access to stable and affordable housing, they are more likely to succeed in other areas of their lives. Children perform better in school, adults can secure and maintain employment, and communities thrive when residents have a safe place to call home. By prioritizing affordable housing initiatives, we are not only addressing homelessness but also building stronger, more resilient communities for the future.

Let's delve deeper into the policy changes needed to make affordable housing a reality for all.

In the quest to address the scarcity of affordable housing as a barrier to solving homelessness, advocating for policy changes is paramount. **Zoning laws** play a crucial role in determining the types of housing that can be built in specific areas. By advocating for reforms in zoning laws, it becomes possible to create more opportunities for affordable housing development. Currently, many zoning regulations restrict the construction of multifamily housing or impose minimum lot sizes that drive up costs. By pushing for more flexible zoning regulations that allow for higher density and mixed-income developments, we can pave the way for a more diverse range of affordable housing options.

Another vital aspect to consider is **rental subsidies**. Many individuals experiencing homelessness or at risk of becoming homeless struggle to afford market-rate rent prices. Rental subsidies can bridge this gap by providing financial assistance to low-income individuals and families, making it possible for them to secure stable housing. By advocating for increased funding for rental subsidy programs and expanding eligibility criteria, we can ensure that more people have access to safe and affordable housing options. This not only addresses immediate housing needs but also helps prevent homelessness in the long run.

Supporting initiatives that aid **non-profit housing developers** is another key strategy in making affordable housing accessible. Non-profit organizations often play a critical role in developing affordable housing projects that prioritize community needs over profit margins. By advocating for policies that provide incentives and resources to non-profit developers, we can encourage the creation of more affordable housing units. Additionally, supporting capacity-building efforts within non-profit organizations can enhance their ability to navigate complex regulatory processes and secure funding for affordable housing projects.

It is essential to understand that these policy changes are not isolated solutions but interconnected components of a comprehensive approach to addressing homelessness through increasing access to affordable housing. By advocating for reforms in zoning laws, rental subsidies, and support for non-profit developers, we can create a more inclusive and sustainable housing landscape that benefits individuals and communities alike.

In conclusion, by championing these policy changes, we can work towards dismantling barriers that hinder access to affordable housing and contribute towards ending homelessness by 2035. Each step taken in advocating for these reforms brings us closer to a future where safe and stable housing is a fundamental right for all individuals, regardless of their income level or background. Let us continue to push for change and build a society where everyone has a place to call home.

Supporting initiatives that aid non-profit housing developers is crucial in the fight to make affordable housing accessible. These developers play a significant role in creating affordable housing options for individuals and families facing homelessness. By providing support to these organizations, we can ensure that more affordable housing units are built, maintained, and made available to those in need. **Non-profit housing developers** often work tirelessly to navigate complex regulations, secure funding, and manage construction projects to bring affordable housing projects to fruition.

One key way to support non-profit housing developers is through **financial assistance**. Providing grants or low-interest loans can help these organizations cover the costs associated with developing affordable housing units. Financial support can also enable non-profit developers to acquire land, purchase materials, and hire skilled labor to complete construction projects within budget constraints. By investing in these developers, we are investing in the future of affordable housing solutions.

Another critical form of support for non-profit housing developers is **technical assistance**. Many of these organizations operate on limited budgets and may not have access to the same level of expertise as larger, for-profit developers. Offering technical assistance in areas such as project management, zoning regulations, and sustainable building practices can help non-profit developers overcome challenges and streamline their operations. By equipping these organizations with the necessary knowledge and skills, we can boost their capacity to create more affordable housing units.

Collaboration is also key when it comes to supporting non-profit housing developers. Partnering with local governments, community organizations, and other stakeholders can amplify the impact of affordable housing initiatives. By working together towards a common goal, we can leverage resources, share best practices, and advocate for policy changes that benefit non-profit developers and the communities they serve. Collaboration fosters a sense of unity and collective responsibility in addressing the affordable housing crisis.

Furthermore, **public awareness** is essential in garnering support for non-profit housing developers. By raising awareness about the importance of their work and the impact of affordable housing projects on communities, we can generate public interest and attract potential donors or volunteers. Spreading the word through social media campaigns, community events, and educational workshops can help shine a light on the valuable contributions of non-profit developers in creating inclusive and sustainable housing solutions.

In conclusion, supporting initiatives that aid non-profit housing developers is a vital component of making affordable housing accessible to all. Through financial assistance, technical support, collaboration, and public awareness efforts, we can empower these organizations to continue their critical work in addressing homelessness and housing insecurity. By rallying behind non-profit developers, we demonstrate our commitment to building a more equitable society where everyone has access to safe and affordable housing options.

Pathway to Possibility: A Step-by-Step Approach to Addressing Homelessness Through Housing

The journey towards making affordable housing accessible and thereby reducing homelessness is both urgent and achievable. By following a structured yet adaptable approach, we can transform the landscape of housing in America and directly tackle the root causes of homelessness.

Step 1: Addressing the Scarcity of Affordable Housing

The stark reality is that affordable housing is not just scarce; it is becoming increasingly difficult to find due to rising costs and stagnant wage growth. This scarcity acts as a major barrier, leaving many vulnerable individuals and families without a stable place to call home. Addressing this begins with understanding the multifaceted challenges, economic, regulatory, and social—that contribute to high housing costs and limited availability.

The impact of these costs is direct and devastating: as housing prices rise, homelessness follows suit. To counteract this, we need robust policies that not only increase the supply of affordable housing but also ensure these homes are accessible to those most in need.

Step 2: Advocating for Policy Changes

Changing policies such as zoning laws and rental subsidies is crucial. These laws often restrict the building of new, affordable housing units that can be remodeled to better meet the demands of growing populations. Examples abound of cities that have successfully reformed their zoning policies, resulting in a significant increase in affordable housing stock.

It's about local solutions as much as national policy—tailoring interventions to fit the unique needs and contexts of different communities. This step requires not just advocacy but active engagement with policymakers, stakeholders, and communities to push for changes that will have real, lasting impacts.

Step 3: Supporting Non-Profit Housing Developers

Non-profit developers play a pivotal role in the affordable housing ecosystem. They often lead the way in innovation and implementation of affordable housing projects but face numerous obstacles, from funding shortages to bureaucratic red tape. Empowering these organizations means providing them with the tools they need—financial, legal, and administrative—to increase their capacity to build and manage affordable housing units.

Celebrating and replicating successful partnerships between non-profit developers and local communities can serve as a model for others. These collaborations not only lead to more housing options but also foster community support and involvement, which are essential for sustainable success.

Moving Forward

This three-step process—addressing scarcity, advocating for change, and supporting non-profits—is not just a plan, but a pathway to possibility. It outlines clear, actionable steps that communities, policymakers, and activists can take to make affordable housing more accessible. Each phase builds upon the last, creating a comprehensive approach to solving one of our nation's most pressing challenges.

By committing to this pathway, we take decisive steps toward not just managing but ending homelessness through the power of housing. Let us move forward with the knowledge that our actions today will shape the communities of tomorrow. Together, we can build a future where everyone has a place to call home.

Chapter 7: Integrating Health: The Role of Mental Care and Addiction Treatment

In the gray wash of early morning, Thomas shuffled through the damp streets of the city, the chill biting through his worn jacket as he navigated his way towards the community center. His mind was a battleground, thoughts clashing with the harsh reality of his circumstances. Homelessness had not been a choice but an inevitability after years of battling undiagnosed bipolar disorder and a descent into alcoholism that washed away his job, his family, and his home.

As he walked, Thomas could still hear the echo of Dr. Simmons' voice from yesterday's appointment at the integrated support program—a rare beacon in his tumultuous life. "It's about treating both your mental health and your addiction together," she had said. He mulled over those words, turning them over like pebbles in a stream, smooth and cool to the touch yet heavy with implication.

Passing by a small park, Thomas watched as children played under the watchful eyes of their parents. The laughter was a stark contrast to the silence in his own life since he had become estranged from his daughter. He wondered if there was a way back to that world—a world where he could belong again.

At the community center, Thomas joined a group session that was already in progress. The room hummed with shared experiences and mutual understanding; it was one place where he didn't feel judged or outcast. As he listened to others speak of their struggles and small victories over addiction and mental health issues, hope flickered within him like a candle in the wind—vulnerable yet persistent.

Later, sitting alone on a bench outside with a sandwich from the center's lunch service, Thomas felt the weight of possibility. Perhaps these integrated programs could be more than just stopgaps; perhaps they could really help someone like him rebuild their life piece by piece. Yet doubt lingered like an old friend, whispering reminders of past failures.

Could this holistic approach truly be enough to change not just his circumstances but also himself? Could it mend not only his present but also bridge back to his lost relationships?

Breaking the Cycle: Why Mental Health and Addiction Services Are Crucial in Solving Homelessness

In our quest to end homelessness by 2035, it is imperative to recognize that many individuals who face homelessness also struggle with mental health issues and substance addiction. The intertwining of these challenges necessitates a comprehensive approach to solutions, one that integrates mental health care and addiction treatment into the broader framework of homelessness interventions. This chapter delves into the critical role that integrated support plays in not only addressing immediate housing needs but also in fostering long-term stability for vulnerable populations.

The Prevalence of Mental Health and Addiction Issues Among the Homeless

Understanding the extent of mental health and addiction issues among homeless populations sets the stage for appreciating the complexity of their needs. Studies consistently show a higher prevalence of mental illness and substance use disorders among those without stable housing compared to the general population. Addressing these issues is not just about treatment; it's about transforming lives and breaking the cycle of homelessness.

Evaluating Integrated Support Programs

Integrated support programs that combine housing solutions

with mental health and addiction services have shown promising results. These programs do more than just provide a roof over one's head; they offer a holistic approach to recovery, helping individuals regain their footing in society. By reviewing various models of integrated care, we can identify best practices and areas for improvement, ensuring that these programs are as effective as possible.

Advocating for Holistic Approaches in Homelessness Interventions

The call for holistic approaches in tackling homelessness is about understanding that stable housing is just one piece of the puzzle. For many, overcoming mental health challenges or breaking free from the grips of addiction is essential to maintaining housing stability. Advocacy for comprehensive interventions is crucial; it ensures that policies and programs are designed to meet the complex needs of those they aim to serve.

Integration is Key to successful outcomes in homelessness interventions. By addressing mental health and addiction alongside housing, we can provide a foundation for lasting stability. This chapter will explore how integrated care models are not only necessary but should be a standard component of all homelessness programs.

Holistic approaches are not just beneficial—they are essential for real change. As we move forward, it's important to advocate for policies that recognize and address the multifaceted nature of homelessness. Only then can we hope to achieve our goal of ending homelessness by 2035.

This conversation about integrating mental health and addiction treatment into homelessness interventions is not just academic; it's about real people and real solutions. By understanding the depth of the issue and recognizing effective strategies, we can make informed decisions that will have a lasting impact on our communities. Let's explore these concepts further, keeping in mind our ultimate goal: a society where everyone has a place to call home.

Homelessness is a complex issue that often intertwines with mental health challenges and substance abuse problems. It is crucial to recognize that many individuals experiencing homelessness also battle mental health issues and addiction. The prevalence of these conditions among the homeless population is significant, underscoring the need for integrated support programs that address these interconnected issues. **Mental health and addiction problems can be major barriers to finding stable housing**, as they can exacerbate other challenges faced by individuals without homes.

Studies have shown that a large percentage of individuals experiencing homelessness struggle with mental health disorders. Conditions such as depression, anxiety, post-traumatic stress disorder (PTSD), and schizophrenia are not uncommon among this vulnerable population. Additionally, substance abuse disorders often co-occur with mental health issues, further complicating the situation. These intertwined challenges make it difficult for individuals to break the cycle of homelessness without targeted support that addresses both their housing needs and their mental well-being.

Integrated support programs that combine mental health and addiction services with housing solutions have shown promising results in helping individuals experiencing homelessness. By addressing the root causes of homelessness, such as untreated mental health conditions and substance abuse, these programs offer a holistic approach to supporting vulnerable individuals. Providing access to counseling, therapy, medication management, and substance abuse treatment can significantly improve outcomes for those seeking to transition out of homelessness.

It is essential to advocate for a comprehensive approach to

addressing homelessness that includes mental health and addiction treatment as integral components. By recognizing the intricate relationship between homelessness, mental health issues, and substance abuse, we can develop more effective interventions that cater to the diverse needs of individuals experiencing homelessness. A one-size-fits-all solution is not sufficient in this context; instead, tailored support programs that consider the unique circumstances of each individual are necessary for long-term success.

Let's delve deeper into the impact of integrated support programs that include mental health and addiction services on individuals experiencing homelessness.

Integrated support programs that encompass mental health and addiction services play a crucial role in addressing the complex needs of individuals experiencing homelessness. These programs go beyond merely providing shelter; they delve into the root causes of homelessness, often intertwined with mental health challenges and substance abuse issues. By offering comprehensive care that includes mental health counseling, addiction treatment, and support services, these programs aim to not only secure housing for individuals but also to equip them with the tools needed to maintain stability in their lives.

One of the key benefits of integrated support programs is their ability to **tackle multiple challenges simultaneously**. Rather than treating mental health, addiction, and homelessness as separate issues, these programs recognize the interconnected nature of these struggles. By addressing them collectively, individuals can experience more holistic healing and progress towards long-term stability. This approach acknowledges that mental health issues and addiction can be significant barriers to obtaining and maintaining housing, emphasizing the need for comprehensive solutions.

In these integrated programs, **mental health professionals** play a vital role in **assessing**, **diagnosing**, and **treating** individuals with mental health conditions. Through therapy sessions, medication management, and personalized care plans, these professionals help individuals navigate their mental health challenges while also addressing any co-occurring substance use disorders. By integrating mental health services into homeless support programs, individuals receive the necessary **emotional support** and **coping mechanisms** to manage their conditions effectively.

Addiction treatment services are another essential component of integrated support programs for individuals experiencing homelessness. Substance abuse can often exacerbate or stem from underlying mental health issues, creating a cycle that hinders progress towards stable housing. By providing access to addiction treatment resources such as detoxification services, counseling, and support groups, these programs offer individuals the opportunity to address their substance use disorders in a supportive environment.

Moreover, integrated support programs often incorporate **case management services** to ensure that individuals receive comprehensive care tailored to their unique needs. Case managers work closely with clients to develop personalized care plans, connect them with necessary resources, monitor their progress, and provide ongoing support. This individualized approach is critical in addressing the complex challenges that individuals facing homelessness may encounter.

By evaluating the effectiveness of integrated support programs that include mental health and addiction services, we gain valuable insights into the impact of holistic care on homeless populations. Research has shown that these programs not only increase housing stability but also lead to improvements in mental health outcomes and reductions in substance use. The success of such initiatives underscores the importance of taking a comprehensive approach to addressing homelessness by integrating mental health and addiction services into support programs.

As we advocate for holistic approaches in homelessness

interventions, it becomes clear that prioritizing mental health and addiction treatment is essential for achieving sustainable solutions. By recognizing the interconnected nature of these issues and providing integrated support that addresses them comprehensively, we can make significant strides towards ending homelessness by 2035.

Integrated Support Framework for Homelessness Interventions

In the realm of homelessness interventions, an integrated support framework is crucial for addressing the complex needs of individuals experiencing homelessness. This framework encompasses a holistic approach that combines mental health care and addiction treatment with housing solutions to provide comprehensive support. Let's delve into the components of this framework to understand how each element contributes to the overall goal of helping individuals achieve stability and well-being.

Universal Screening and Assessment

Universal screening for mental health and addiction issues among the homeless population serves as the foundational step in identifying individuals in need of specialized support. By conducting thorough assessments, service providers can tailor interventions to address the specific needs of each individual effectively. This component ensures that no one slips through the cracks and that everyone receives the appropriate level of care.

Immediate and Continuous Access to Treatment Services

Immediate access to mental health and addiction treatment services is essential for preventing crises and supporting individuals in their journey towards recovery. Timely interventions can mitigate the negative impacts of untreated conditions, enhancing overall well-being and stability. Moreover, **continuous access** ensures that individuals receive ongoing support to maintain their progress and prevent relapse, fostering long-term positive outcomes.

Coordination Between Housing Services and Healthcare Providers

Coordination between housing services and healthcare providers is key to delivering integrated care that addresses both medical and social needs. Collaboration between these entities facilitates seamless transitions for individuals moving from homelessness into stable housing situations. By working together, housing providers and healthcare professionals can create a supportive environment conducive to recovery and sustained wellness.

Personalized Care Plans and Peer Support

Personalized care plans cater to the unique needs of each individual, taking into account their mental health, addiction history, and personal goals. These tailored plans ensure that interventions are relevant and effective, maximizing outcomes for each person. Additionally, **peer support** plays a vital role in providing empathy, understanding, and encouragement from individuals with lived experience, fostering a sense of community and belonging essential for recovery.

Community-Based Services

Community-based services offer a continuum of care beyond clinical settings, engaging individuals in their local communities for ongoing support. These services include outreach programs, peer-led initiatives, vocational training, and recreational activities aimed at promoting social inclusion and enhancing quality of life. By integrating community resources into the support network, individuals can access diverse forms of assistance tailored to their holistic well-being.

Key Performance Indicators for Evaluation

Key performance indicators such as reductions in emergency department visits, improvements in housing stability, and enhanced well-being serve as measurable outcomes for evaluating the effectiveness of integrated support programs. These metrics guide program evaluation efforts, allowing stakeholders to assess impact, identify areas for improvement, and make data-driven decisions to enhance service delivery.

Policy Support and Infrastructure Development

Policy support is essential for scaling integrated programs that combine mental health care, addiction treatment, and housing solutions effectively. Advocacy efforts aimed at securing funding, shaping legislation, and promoting best practices in service delivery are critical for sustaining long-term interventions. Moreover, **infrastructure development**, including robust referral networks, data-sharing systems, and interdisciplinary collaboration mechanisms are necessary to ensure seamless coordination among service providers across different sectors.

In conclusion, an integrated support framework that combines mental health care and addiction treatment with housing solutions offers a comprehensive approach to addressing homelessness effectively. By incorporating universal screening processes, immediate access to treatment services, coordinated care plans, peer support networks, community-based services, performance indicators for evaluation, as well as policy support and infrastructure development initiatives, sustainable interventions can be developed that prioritize individual well-being while working towards ending homelessness by 2035.

Integrating mental health and addiction treatment into the fabric of support programs for the homeless is not just beneficial, it's crucial. Many individuals experiencing homelessness battle with mental health issues and substance addiction, two significant barriers that can prevent them from securing and maintaining stable housing. By addressing these challenges in tandem with housing solutions, we significantly increase the likelihood of successful, long-term outcomes.

Understanding that these are not isolated issues but interconnected ones is fundamental. When we look at homelessness through a holistic lens, we see not just a lack of shelter but a complex web of personal and systemic challenges. Programs that merge mental health care and addiction treatment with housing services are not just treating symptoms; they are addressing root causes. This integrated approach fosters a more sustainable recovery and reintegration into society.

Consider the power of a supportive environment where an individual is not only given a key to an apartment but is also supported through counseling and tailored addiction services. Here, the chance of relapse into homelessness diminishes significantly. This isn't merely hopeful thinking; it's backed by numerous studies that show integrated support systems lead to better retention of housing and improved overall well-being.

The evidence is clear: when care is coordinated and comprehensive, the results are transformative. This approach does not simplify the problem; rather, it acknowledges and addresses the complexity of the individual's needs. It's about rebuilding lives, not just providing temporary shelters.

Moreover, this integration is a reflection of a compassionate society that sees beyond the immediate. It represents a commitment to rebuilding lives thoroughly, not superficially patching over issues of homelessness. In doing so, we not only help individuals but also contribute to the health of our communities.

Let's carry this understanding forward. Let's ensure that every intervention, every policy, and every program designed to tackle homelessness includes these critical components. By doing so, we not only enhance the effectiveness of our efforts but also affirm our collective responsibility towards creating a just and caring society.

In weaving together mental health care and addiction treatment with housing services, we are not just offering a lifeline; we are providing a foundation upon which individuals can rebuild their lives. It's an approach that respects the dignity of each person and recognizes their potential to overcome challenges and flourish. Let this be the cornerstone of our strategy as we move forward in our quest to end homelessness.

Chapter 8: Power in Unity: Community Engagement in Homelessness Programs

In the early hours of a brisk autumn morning, the city began to stir under a canopy of fading stars. The streets, lined with ancient oaks, whispered tales of countless sunrises and sunsets as they shook off the night's chill. Here, in this urban sprawl where nature met concrete, Martin found himself pacing the length of an old iron bridge that arched over a slow-moving river. His breath formed little clouds that danced away into the dawn.

Martin was a man of modest height with sharp eyes that seemed to take in more than they let on. Once homeless, he had climbed out from under the city's harsh clutches through sheer will and a bit of luck involving an outreach program led by people who once stood where he did. Now, as a community organizer, he was wrestling with how best to involve local residents in developing solutions for homelessness—solutions that would not only serve but also empower.

As he walked, his mind buzzed with thoughts of yesterday's meeting where tensions had flared. Some residents felt unheard; others were skeptical about new initiatives. "How can I bridge these gaps?" he wondered silently. His leather shoes clacked against the pavement rhythmically, echoing his turbulent thoughts.

A jogger brushed past him, her ponytail flicking like a metronome against her back—a reminder of life's steady pulse amidst chaos. Martin watched her disappear into the morning mist that hung over the river like a soft veil. He thought about how each person's experience with homelessness is like mist; unique and ephemeral yet pervasive.

Turning his gaze back to the horizon where light now painted the sky in strokes of pink and gold, Martin recalled stories from individuals who had lived on these very streets—stories of despair transformed into hope and resilience through communal support and tailored interventions. These narratives fueled his commitment but also his doubt: Was he truly fostering change or merely applying temporary fixes?

A sudden gust sent leaves swirling around him as if urging him to move forward with resolve. The scent of damp earth rose from below—the riverbank nurturing life in its shadowy waters just as communities could nurture those lost within their folds.

Martin stopped at the mid-span of the bridge and looked down at the flowing water below, reflecting on how every small effort contributed to larger ripples across this human ecosystem. Could he find a way to channel these individual experiences into a collective force for good?

As dawn broke fully over the cityscape before him—buildings aglow with golden light—he knew there was no turning back from this challenge laid out at his feet by fate or circumstance or perhaps both.

How can we harness individual stories and community wisdom to not just address but solve deeper social issues like homelessness?

Can We Truly End Homelessness Without Community Power?

The journey towards eradicating homelessness in America by 2035 is not just a policy challenge; it is a community imperative. **Engagement at the local level** is vital because it taps into the very fabric of the places affected by homelessness. This chapter explores how involving community members—particularly those who have lived experiences of homelessness—can transform good intentions into effective, enduring solutions.

The Crucial Role of Community Involvement

At its core, community involvement in tackling homelessness ensures that solutions are not only designed but are lived and breathed within the very communities they aim to help. **Local insights** provide invaluable perspectives that can dramatically tailor and improve the effectiveness of interventions. When people who live, work, and play in a community come together to address such a pressing issue, the solutions devised are more likely to be embraced and sustained over time.

Strategies for Effective Engagement

Engaging communities, especially those directly impacted by homelessness, requires thoughtful strategies that respect and harness their insights. This chapter will discuss various methods to foster genuine participation from community members. From town hall meetings to participatory design processes, it's about creating spaces where voices can be heard and valued equally. The goal is to move beyond mere consultation to active co-creation of solutions.

Learning from Success Stories

Analyzing case studies where community involvement has led to successful outcomes provides concrete examples of the power of collective action. These stories not only inspire but also serve as practical guides that can be adapted and replicated elsewhere. Whether it's a small town that rallied to provide safe housing options or a city that integrated homelessness prevention into its school system, these examples show what's possible when communities lead the way.

In this chapter, we will delve into these three key areas with clarity and purpose. The aim is to underscore the undeniable truth that sustainable success in homelessness programs demands deep-rooted community involvement. By examining effective strategies and learning from past successes, we can better understand how to mobilize communities towards achieving our national goal.

The insights provided here are meant not just to inform but also to inspire action. As we navigate through this chapter, remember that every community holds unique keys to solving its challenges. Engaging with them isn't just beneficial—it's essential for creating lasting change in the landscape of American homelessness.

Through this exploration, it becomes clear: ending homelessness is not solely about building more shelters or creating more programs; it's about building stronger communities. And when we harness this collective power responsibly and creatively, we unlock potential solutions that are as diverse and resilient as the communities themselves.

So let's embark on this critical conversation together, exploring how united efforts can lead us closer to a future where no American has to experience homelessness again.

Community involvement is not just a nice-to-have element in homelessness programs; it is a crucial component of their success. **Engaging local communities ensures that solutions are tailored to meet specific needs**, taking into account the unique challenges and resources of each area. When community members, especially those who have experienced homelessness themselves, are actively involved in the design and implementation of programs, the outcomes are more likely to be sustainable and effective in the long term.

Local communities hold valuable insights into the root causes of homelessness in their area. By involving residents, service providers, businesses, and local leaders in the decision-making process, programs can be more targeted and responsive to the actual needs of the population experiencing homelessness. **This collaborative approach leads to more holistic solutions** that address not only housing but also factors like mental health support, job training, and access to healthcare.

When communities are engaged in developing homelessness

solutions, there is a greater sense of ownership and accountability. **Residents become invested in the success of the programs**, leading to increased support and participation. This sense of ownership fosters a culture of collective responsibility where everyone plays a role in addressing homelessness rather than relying solely on government or nonprofit organizations.

Involving local communities also helps to break down stigmas and misconceptions surrounding homelessness. **When individuals have the opportunity to interact with those experiencing homelessness**, they gain a better understanding of the complex issues at play. This firsthand experience can lead to greater empathy and support for initiatives aimed at ending homelessness.

Community engagement fosters innovation by bringing together diverse perspectives and ideas. Local residents often have creative solutions based on their knowledge of the community's strengths and challenges. By tapping into this collective wisdom, programs can identify new approaches that may not have been considered otherwise.

Let's delve deeper into strategies for engaging community members, especially those with firsthand experience, to create impactful homelessness programs that truly make a difference.

Community engagement is not just a buzzword; it is the cornerstone of successful homelessness programs. Involving local community members, especially those who have firsthand experience with homelessness, is essential for creating effective and sustainable solutions. **Engaging individuals who have walked in the shoes of the homeless population brings invaluable insights and perspectives to the table**. These individuals can provide unique insights into the challenges faced by the homeless, helping to tailor programs to meet their specific needs.

One powerful strategy for engaging community members is through participatory decision-making processes. This approach involves actively involving community members in the planning, implementation, and evaluation of homelessness programs. By including those directly impacted by homelessness in decision-making processes, programs become more responsive to the real needs of the community. **Empowering individuals to be part of the solution fosters a sense of ownership and commitment**, leading to more sustainable outcomes.

Another effective strategy is to create opportunities for peer support and mentorship within the community. People who have successfully transitioned out of homelessness can serve as mentors to those currently experiencing homelessness, offering guidance, support, and hope. **Peer support programs not only provide practical assistance but also foster a sense of belonging and connection** within the community, reducing isolation and stigma.

Building strong partnerships with local organizations, businesses, and government agencies is also crucial for effective community engagement. Collaborating with a diverse range of stakeholders ensures that homelessness programs are comprehensive, well-coordinated, and sustainable. **By working together towards a common goal, communities can leverage their collective resources and expertise to address homelessness from multiple angles**.

Education and awareness campaigns play a vital role in engaging the broader community in addressing homelessness. By raising awareness about the root causes of homelessness, challenging stereotypes, and dispelling myths, communities can foster empathy and understanding. **Empowering individuals with knowledge helps break down barriers and build a more compassionate and supportive community**.

Listening is key to effective community engagement. Creating platforms for open dialogue, feedback sessions, and town hall meetings allows community members to voice their concerns, ideas, and suggestions. **By actively listening to the voices of the**

community, program developers can gain valuable insights that inform decision-making processes and improve program outcomes.

In conclusion, **engaging local communities in developing homelessness solutions is not just a nice-to-have; it is a must-have for creating impactful and sustainable change**. By leveraging the unique insights, experiences, and resources within communities, we can design programs that are responsive to local needs, inclusive of diverse perspectives, and ultimately effective in ending homelessness by 2035.

Community involvement has time and again proven to be the key ingredient in creating sustainable solutions to homelessness. By actively engaging local communities in the design and implementation of programs, we ensure that the initiatives are tailored to address specific needs and challenges faced by those experiencing homelessness. Let's delve into a few case studies where community involvement has led to remarkable outcomes, showcasing the power of unity in tackling homelessness.

In Portland, Oregon, a community-driven initiative called "Dignity Village" emerged as a response to the lack of affordable housing options for individuals experiencing homelessness. This self-governed community provides transitional housing and support services, all managed by its residents. **Through collective effort and shared responsibility**, Dignity Village has not only provided shelter but also fostered a sense of belonging and empowerment among its residents.

Moving across the country to New York City, the Jericho Project stands as a testament to the impact of engaging community members with lived experience in homelessness programs. By incorporating input from individuals who have overcome homelessness themselves, the Jericho Project has been able to design comprehensive support services that address not only housing needs but also mental health, employment, and social integration. **The firsthand knowledge and insight** of those who have walked the path of homelessness are invaluable in shaping effective solutions.

In Salt Lake City, Utah, the Housing First program gained traction due to strong community support and involvement. This innovative approach prioritizes providing stable housing as a first step, followed by additional support services tailored to individual needs. **By rallying together**, local organizations, government agencies, and community members have successfully reduced chronic homelessness in the city. The collaborative spirit and shared commitment to ending homelessness have been instrumental in achieving lasting results.

In each of these case studies, one common thread emerges: the power of unity in driving positive change. When communities come together with a shared goal of addressing homelessness, remarkable transformations can take place. **By harnessing collective wisdom** and mobilizing resources effectively, we can create sustainable solutions that uplift individuals and strengthen communities as a whole.

These examples serve as beacons of hope and inspiration for communities everywhere facing the challenge of homelessness. They illustrate that progress is possible when we work hand in hand with those most affected by the issue. **Through collaboration** and a deep understanding of local needs, we can pave the way for a future where everyone has a place to call home.

Throughout this discussion, we've seen how the fabric of community involvement can fundamentally enhance the effectiveness of homelessness programs. The engagement of local communities isn't merely a nice-to-have; it's a **crucial component** in crafting solutions that are not only sustainable but also deeply resonant with the needs of those they aim to serve.

By integrating the voices of those who have lived experiences of homelessness, programs gain invaluable insights that lead to more tailored and effective interventions. This approach does more than just solve an issue; it **empowers individuals** and fosters a sense of ownership and responsibility within the community. This is not just about finding temporary shelters or quick fixes but about building long-term strategies that address the root causes of homelessness.

The case studies highlighted earlier bring to light a compelling truth: when communities come together, the impact can be profound and lasting. These examples serve as a testament to the power of collective action and shared responsibility. They are not mere stories; they are roadmaps that show us how engagement can transform good intentions into actionable, sustainable outcomes.

As we move forward, let's carry with us the understanding that every community has a unique set of resources, challenges, and dynamics. There is no one-size-fits-all solution to homelessness, but there is a universal truth in the effectiveness of involving those directly affected. It is their insights that can lead to breakthroughs in how we address this pressing issue.

Engage, listen, and act—these are not just steps but a mantra for driving change. By fostering an environment where every voice can be heard and valued, we are not just addressing homelessness; we are rebuilding lives with dignity and respect.

Let this chapter serve as both a reflection and a call to action. The journey to ending homelessness is complex and challenging, but it is also filled with opportunities for communities to demonstrate their resilience and compassion. By working together, learning from each other, and committing to inclusive, community-driven approaches, we can create a future where homelessness is no longer a reality but a memory.

As we continue to explore the possibilities and apply the lessons learned, remember that every small effort counts, and each community member can be a catalyst for real change. The road ahead is built through perseverance, collaboration, and an unwavering belief in the power of unity. Let's step forward with confidence and commitment to make that difference.

Chapter 9: Flexible Frameworks: Adapting Strategies to Local Needs

In the dim light of the early morning, Thomas walked through the quiet streets of his small town, his breath visible in the crisp air. The chill wrapped around him like a cloak as he passed by empty storefronts and silent houses. His mind was occupied with a pressing concern that had taken root deep within him, a problem that seemed to grow heavier with each step he took.

Thomas was a city planner, and lately, his town had been facing an increasing issue with homelessness. The streets where he now walked were becoming more populated at night with those who had no place to call home. As he moved through the town square, he noticed remnants from the night before: a tattered blanket tucked into a doorway, a worn-out shoe lying forgotten near the bench. These sights stirred a mixture of frustration and empathy in him.

He thought about the meeting he had later that day with other town officials. They were to discuss strategies to address this growing problem. Thomas knew that any plan they came up with needed to be both adaptable and scalable; what worked for one community might not work for another, and as their town grew, so too might their homeless population.

As he turned down Maple Street, Thomas recalled a conference he attended last year where various adaptable models of homelessness strategies were discussed. There was talk of tiny home villages in one city and converted shipping containers in another. Each solution was tailored to fit specific community needs and resources available.

The bakery on the corner was just opening as Thomas approached, its warm glow inviting in the cool dawn. He paused outside, watching as Mrs. Avery inside arranged loaves of bread behind the window display. Her movements were methodical and comforting—a stark contrast to the turmoil in his own thoughts.

"Morning, Thomas!" she called out as she spotted him outside her shop.

"Good morning, Mrs. Avery," Thomas replied, managing a smile as he stepped inside, where the scent of fresh bread enveloped him.

As they exchanged pleasantries about the weather and local news, Thomas' thoughts drifted back to his problem at hand. He wondered if perhaps integrating job training programs within housing solutions could offer both immediate relief and long-term benefits to those affected by homelessness in their community.

Leaving the bakery with a loaf under his arm for breakfast, Thomas felt slightly more hopeful but still uncertain about how best to proceed. The challenge was daunting but not insurmountable if they could tailor their approach carefully.

Why is it crucial for communities like Thomas's to consider both immediate needs and future growth when devising solutions for homelessness?

Tailoring Solutions for Every Community: How Local Adaptation Can End Homelessness

When envisioning a future where homelessness is a relic of the past, it's crucial to recognize that **one size does not fit all**. The varied tapestry of America—from bustling urban centers to serene rural landscapes—demands a mosaic of strategies, each uniquely suited to its environment. This chapter delves into why adaptable and scalable frameworks are not just beneficial but essential in crafting effective solutions to homelessness across diverse communities.

Homelessness, as a social issue, manifests differently from one locale to another, influenced by factors such as economic conditions, availability of resources, and community norms. Thus, strategies that work well in one city might not be effective in another. Recognizing this complexity is the first step toward developing solutions that are both flexible enough to be modified as per local needs and robust enough to be scaled up to meet national objectives.

The Essence of Adaptability and Scalability

To set the stage, let's define what makes a strategy both adaptable and scalable. *Adaptability* refers to the ability of a program to adjust to the changing dynamics or unique challenges of a particular area without losing its effectiveness. *Scalability*, on the other hand, ensures that a small local success can be expanded or replicated in other regions, multiplying the impact of the original model. Together, these qualities ensure that strategies are resilient and responsive—key attributes for any initiative aiming to tackle the complex issue of homelessness.

Learning from Diverse Models

In our journey through various models that epitomize adaptability, we will explore how different locales have tailored their approaches to meet specific needs. From housing-first initiatives in urban settings to community-based prevention programs in rural areas, these models provide a blueprint for what can be achieved when strategies are molded to fit local contexts. Each model offers valuable lessons on integrating flexibility into program design and execution.

The Power of Tailored Approaches

Moreover, the discussion will extend into how these adaptable models address distinct community challenges—be it through policy innovation, resource allocation, or collaborative efforts. Tailoring approaches not only enhance efficacy but also foster community ownership and engagement—a crucial element in sustaining long-term success.

By examining these elements closely, this chapter aims not only to inform but also to inspire action. The goal is clear: equip policymakers, practitioners, and communities with the knowledge and tools they need to effectively adapt their strategies against homelessness. In doing so, we pave the way for more resilient communities capable of confronting and overcoming this challenge.

Through this exploration, it becomes evident that flexibility is not merely an optional add-on but rather a fundamental aspect of any successful strategy against homelessness. By fostering environments where adaptability is ingrained in every step of solution formulation and implementation, we move closer to a future where homelessness is no longer a defining feature of any community in America.

Let us engage with these insights with an open mind and a committed heart—ready to learn, adapt, and ultimately succeed in eradicating homelessness from our nation by 2035.

Homelessness is not a uniform issue; it manifests differently in various communities, necessitating adaptable and scalable strategies to effectively combat it. **Adaptable strategies** are crucial because what works in one city may not be as effective in another due to differences in demographics, resources, and local conditions. **Scalability** is equally important to ensure that successful initiatives can be expanded to reach more individuals in need without losing their effectiveness.

To develop successful homelessness strategies, it is essential to understand the unique challenges faced by different communities. Factors such as **housing availability**, **economic opportunities**, **mental health services**, and **support networks** all play a role in shaping the experience of homelessness in a particular area. By tailoring interventions to address these specific needs, organizations and policymakers can create more impactful solutions.

Flexibility is key when implementing strategies to address

homelessness. What works in a rural community may not be suitable for an urban setting, and vice versa. **Adaptable frameworks** allow for customization based on the local context, ensuring that interventions are relevant and effective. This approach also encourages innovation and creativity in problem-solving, as solutions can be tailored to fit the unique circumstances of each community.

Moreover, scalable strategies are essential for making a significant impact on homelessness at a broader level. While pilot programs and small-scale initiatives are valuable for testing new ideas, true progress comes from being able to replicate and expand successful models. **Scalability** enables organizations to reach more people in need and create lasting change by implementing proven strategies on a larger scale.

By combining adaptability with scalability, communities can develop comprehensive approaches to addressing homelessness that are both effective and sustainable. This dual focus allows for targeted interventions that meet the specific needs of individuals experiencing homelessness while also building a foundation for long-term success. **Adaptable and scalable strategies** provide the flexibility to adjust tactics as needed while maintaining a focus on achieving the overarching goal of ending homelessness.

Ready to explore how adaptable models are being used in diverse settings? Let's delve into the innovative approaches that are making a difference in communities across the country.

In addressing homelessness, it's crucial to recognize the diverse needs of different communities and the necessity of adaptable models to effectively combat this issue. **One size does not fit all** when it comes to homelessness solutions. What works in a bustling urban center may not be as effective in a rural community. Therefore, it's essential to explore various adaptable models that have been successfully implemented in diverse settings to understand how tailored approaches can make a significant impact.

Homelessness is not a monolithic problem, and its root causes and manifestations can vary greatly from one region to another. For example, strategies that focus on affordable housing initiatives might be more suitable for densely populated cities grappling with high rent prices, while programs that address mental health and addiction issues could be more relevant in areas where these factors contribute significantly to homelessness.

Flexibility is key when designing strategies to tackle homelessness. By examining successful models implemented in different contexts, we can gain valuable insights into what works best under specific circumstances. For instance, a program that combines job training with transitional housing might be the right approach for helping homeless individuals reintegrate into the workforce in certain areas, while a focus on family reunification could be more beneficial in communities where family breakdown is a primary cause of homelessness.

Adaptable frameworks allow for innovation and customization, enabling communities to address their unique challenges effectively. By learning from successful initiatives across various settings, we can identify best practices and tailor them to suit local needs. This approach not only fosters creativity but also encourages collaboration among stakeholders to create sustainable solutions.

It's essential to consider the scalability of these models as well. While localized strategies are crucial for addressing immediate needs, scalable solutions are necessary for making a broader impact and achieving long-term goals. By examining adaptable models that have been successfully scaled up, communities can learn how to expand their efforts effectively without losing sight of their core objectives.

By exploring adaptable models used in diverse settings, we can uncover innovative approaches that have proven effective in addressing homelessness from multiple angles. Whether it's through partnerships with local businesses, government agencies, or nonprofit organizations, these models demonstrate the power of collaboration in creating sustainable solutions. By understanding how different communities have adapted their strategies to meet local needs, we can gain valuable insights into what works best in specific contexts and apply those lessons to drive change on a larger scale.

The key takeaway is that flexibility and scalability are essential when developing strategies to combat homelessness. By embracing adaptable frameworks and learning from successful models implemented in diverse settings, communities can effectively address the complex challenges of homelessness while working towards long-term solutions. This approach not only empowers communities to tailor interventions to their unique circumstances but also lays the groundwork for a coordinated nationwide effort to end homelessness by 2035.

Evaluation Framework: A Methodological Approach

In developing tailored approaches to address homelessness in diverse communities, incorporating an Evaluation Framework is crucial. This framework serves as a methodological guide to adapt and scale homelessness solutions effectively based on local needs. By establishing criteria for evaluating interventions, such as cost-effectiveness, impact on homelessness rates, quality of life improvements, and community satisfaction, this framework ensures that strategies are not only responsive but also measurable in their outcomes.

Baseline Data Collection

The first stage of the Evaluation Framework involves **baseline data collection** to understand the unique context of each community. This step is essential for identifying specific challenges, resources, and demographics that influence the prevalence of homelessness in a particular area. By gathering accurate data, stakeholders can make informed decisions about which interventions will be most effective in addressing local needs.

Criteria Matrix for Intervention Selection

Following data collection, the next step is to use a **criteria matrix** that aligns with specific community needs and available resources. This matrix helps decision-makers evaluate potential interventions against predetermined criteria to ensure that selected strategies are not only suitable but also feasible within the given context. By aligning interventions with identified needs, this step increases the likelihood of successful outcomes.

Implementation Phases and Stakeholder Engagement

The framework outlines clear **implementation phases**, emphasizing the importance of pilot testing, stakeholder engagement, and iterative learning. Pilot testing allows for adjustments to be made before full-scale implementation, reducing risks and optimizing resources. Involving stakeholders ensures that interventions are culturally sensitive and supported by those directly impacted by homelessness.

Robust Feedback Mechanism

An essential component of the Evaluation Framework is a **robust feedback mechanism** that captures outcomes, stakeholder input, and lessons learned throughout the process. This feedback loop enables continuous refinement of strategies based on real-time data and stakeholder feedback. By incorporating this element, the framework promotes adaptability and responsiveness to changing community needs.

Visual Representations for Clarity

Visual representations within the framework can elucidate the cyclical nature of assessment, adaptation, implementation, and evaluation. These visuals help stakeholders understand the dynamic process of developing tailored solutions to combat homelessness effectively. By providing a visual roadmap of key steps in the framework, complex processes become more accessible and easier to follow.

The Evaluation Framework offers a data-driven, participatory approach to addressing homelessness by tailoring solutions to meet diverse community needs. Through systematic evaluation and adaptation based on local contexts, this framework ensures that interventions remain relevant and effective over time. By emphasizing stakeholder engagement, iterative learning, and continuous refinement, this model provides a structured yet flexible approach to combating homelessness at a local level.

As we've explored in this chapter, the variability in homelessness across different regions of America calls for **strategies that are not only effective but also flexible and scalable**. This adaptability is crucial because it allows each community to tailor solutions to meet its unique needs while aligning with broader national goals.

Imagine a toolset carefully crafted to be both robust and versatile. In much the same way, our strategies to combat homelessness must function. They need to be robust enough to tackle the broad spectrum of issues that lead to homelessness, yet versatile enough to adapt to local socio-economic conditions, cultural nuances, and resource availabilities.

The importance of adaptable models cannot be overstated. From urban centers dealing with high housing costs to rural areas where resources are sparse, the challenge varies significantly. We have seen models that prioritize rapid rehousing in cities while others focus on community integration and support systems in less populated areas. Each model, when applied thoughtfully, reflects a deep understanding of the local context, ensuring that solutions are not just applied but are embedded within the community.

Moreover, *tailoring approaches to different community needs* is not merely a logistical necessity but a moral imperative. It underscores a commitment to addressing homelessness in a manner that respects and responds to the dignity and diversity of all individuals affected by it. This tailored approach ensures that no one is left behind or overlooked because of their geographical or socio-economic status.

This chapter has laid down a framework that champions flexibility and scalability in strategies to end homelessness. As we move forward, let us carry with us the understanding that **our approach must be as dynamic and diverse as the communities we aim to serve**. With this mindset, we edge closer towards a future where homelessness is not just managed but eradicated.

In the next chapter, we will build on these ideas, exploring how these adaptable frameworks can be supported by policy changes at various levels of government. This is where strategy meets action, ensuring that our plans do not just stay on paper but leap into life, bringing about real change across the nation.

Chapter 10: The Power of Data: Making Informed Adjustments for Long-term Success

In the dim light of early morning, Thomas strolled through the quiet streets of the city, his breath visible in the chill air. He was a man tasked with a burden that weighed heavily on his heart—reducing homelessness through informed strategies and data-driven decisions. His hands were shoved deep into his pockets, feeling the cold bite at his fingers as he passed by shadowed doorways where figures huddled under ragged blankets.

The city was just beginning to stir, a bakery nearby releasing the scent of fresh bread into the air, mingling with the less pleasant odors that came from neglected corners. Thomas paused outside an old building slated for renovation into affordable housing. He thought about the data he had reviewed just yesterday—numbers that told stories of loss, resilience, and rare triumphs. It was this data that guided each decision he made, aiming to turn statistics back into human lives with dignity.

Inside a small café, warmed by the hum of quiet conversations and clinking dishes, Thomas sipped his coffee and spread out his papers filled with graphs and charts. Each line and curve represented a part of his ongoing challenge: to adjust strategies in real time based on emerging patterns and needs. The waitress noticed his focused expression and offered a refill of his coffee without interrupting his thoughts.

He remembered a recent success story—a program adjustment made possible by analyzing shelter occupancy rates and average durations of stay, which led to an increased focus on mental health services at key locations. This shift had reduced repeat homelessness significantly in those areas, a small victory in the larger battle.

As he walked back towards his office, Thomas stopped to chat with Marianne, who managed one of the local shelters. She shared anecdotes from the ground—how recent changes were affecting those they aimed to help—and her feedback would be invaluable for refining their approach further.

Thomas looked up at the sky; it promised rain later. His mind returned to those charts spread out across his table back in the café. How many more adjustments would be needed? How much data would be enough to truly make a difference?

Would they ever reach a point where their strategies no longer require constant change?

Harnessing Insights from Data to Propel Us Forward

Imagine navigating a ship through uncharted waters without a map or compass. This is the challenge faced when addressing homelessness without the aid of robust data. As we near the concluding discussions of our blueprint for ending homelessness by 2035, it's crucial to emphasize how informed adjustments, driven by empirical data, are not just beneficial but essential. Data acts as our compass in this complex endeavor, guiding us through the fog of uncertainty and allowing for strategic recalibrations that steer us towards our destination: the eradication of homelessness in America.

The Role of Data in Dynamic Environments

The landscape of homelessness is as dynamic as it is diverse, influenced by economic shifts, policy changes, and social trends. In this context, static solutions are often inadequate. **Data serves as a critical tool** that allows us to monitor the effectiveness of our strategies continuously. By understanding which initiatives deliver desired outcomes and which fall short, we can iterate and evolve our approaches effectively. This chapter will delve into how data not only measures success but also highlights areas needing refinement or a complete overhaul.

Building Robust Mechanisms for Data Collection

Collecting data might sound straightforward, but the devil lies in the details. What types of data should we collect? How do we ensure it's both relevant and reliable? These questions are pivotal. We'll explore established mechanisms for data collection that have been successfully implemented in various regions. These systems not only gather quantitative data like numbers and percentages but also qualitative insights that shed light on the human experiences behind the statistics.

Learning from Success Stories

Real-world examples illuminate paths and pitfalls alike. Discussing case studies where data-driven strategies have led to significant reductions in homelessness provides not just inspiration but a practical framework that other regions can adapt and implement. These narratives underscore the potency of being responsive rather than reactive—adjusting strategies based on what the data tells us about current needs and future trends.

In synthesizing these elements, this chapter aims to weave together the overarching themes presented throughout this book. We've discussed at length the systemic causes of homelessness, its financial implications, and various successful interventions. Here, we underscore that **the journey doesn't end with implementation**; continual adjustment informed by rigorous data analysis ensures these solutions remain effective as circumstances evolve.

By equipping ourselves with comprehensive, actionable plans tailored to specific contexts—underpinned by ongoing data analysis—we empower communities across America not just to tackle but to solve homelessness. This approach does not simplify the complexity of the issue; instead, it harnesses that complexity as a dynamic resource from which to draw strength and adaptability.

Through this discourse, we aim not only to inform but to inspire action that is both thoughtful and impactful. By understanding how to leverage data effectively, stakeholders at all levels can participate in a coordinated effort that matches the scale of our ambition—to end homelessness decisively by 2035.

Data plays a crucial role in the ongoing battle against homelessness. It serves as a compass, guiding us through the complex landscape of social issues and pointing us towards effective solutions. By monitoring and analyzing data, we can assess the impact of our programs, identify areas for improvement, and make informed adjustments to ensure long-term success in our mission to end homelessness. Without data, we would be navigating blindly, unable to measure progress or steer our efforts in the right direction.

Data is not just numbers on a spreadsheet; it tells the stories of individuals experiencing homelessness. Each data point represents a person in need, a life that could be transformed by our actions. By collecting and analyzing data, we gain insights into the root causes of homelessness, the effectiveness of our interventions, and the evolving needs of those we aim to serve. It humanizes the issue, reminding us that behind every statistic is a unique individual deserving of dignity and support.

Monitoring data allows us to track progress and identify trends in homelessness rates, demographics, and contributing factors. It enables us to measure the effectiveness of our programs and initiatives, highlighting what works and what needs improvement. Data empowers us to make evidence-based decisions, steering our efforts towards strategies that yield tangible results. Without this information, we would be working blindly, unable to gauge the impact of our interventions or adapt to changing circumstances.

Data-driven adjustments are essential for long-term success in combating homelessness. As societal factors shift and new challenges emerge, our strategies must evolve to meet the evolving needs of those experiencing homelessness. By constantly monitoring data and making informed adjustments based on empirical evidence, we can ensure that our efforts remain relevant and effective over time. This dynamic approach is key to sustaining progress and ultimately achieving our goal of ending homelessness by 2035.

Continue reading to explore how mechanisms for collecting and analyzing data can evaluate program effectiveness in combating homelessness effectively.

Continual data-driven adjustments are essential in the fight against homelessness. **Collecting and analyzing data** allows us to evaluate the effectiveness of our programs and make informed decisions about where adjustments are needed. Without this critical step, we risk implementing strategies that may not address the root causes of homelessness or provide the necessary support for those in need. By diving into the data, we can gain valuable insights that guide us towards more impactful solutions.

Mechanisms for collecting and analyzing data come in various forms, from surveys and interviews with individuals experiencing homelessness to tracking metrics on program outcomes. Each piece of information gathered contributes to a more comprehensive understanding of the issue at hand. By utilizing both quantitative and qualitative data, we can paint a vivid picture of the challenges faced by those without stable housing and identify patterns that inform our next steps.

When it comes to **evaluating program effectiveness**, data is our compass. It tells us whether we are on the right track or if adjustments are necessary to achieve our goals. Monitoring key performance indicators allows us to measure progress over time and make real-time corrections when needed. Without this feedback loop, we risk investing time and resources into programs that may not be yielding the desired results.

Analyzing data to evaluate program effectiveness is not just about numbers; it's about understanding the stories behind the statistics. Data can reveal trends, disparities, and areas of success that might otherwise go unnoticed. By digging deep into the numbers, we can uncover insights that shape more targeted interventions and ensure that our efforts are making a tangible difference in the lives of those experiencing homelessness.

In the realm of homelessness initiatives, success hinges on our ability to adapt based on empirical evidence. **Making data-driven adjustments** is not a one-time task but an ongoing process that requires vigilance and flexibility. As we navigate the complexities of addressing homelessness, our willingness to pivot based on what the data tells us will ultimately determine our long-term impact.

The power of data lies in its ability to illuminate pathways forward. **By leveraging data to evaluate program effectiveness**, we can steer our efforts towards greater efficacy and sustainability. Through careful analysis and informed decision-making, we can refine our strategies to better serve individuals experiencing homelessness and move closer towards our shared goal of ending homelessness by 2035.

In conclusion, collecting and analyzing data is not just a technical exercise; it is a cornerstone of effective homelessness initiatives. **By embracing data-driven adjustments**, we empower ourselves to make meaningful changes that have a lasting impact on individuals, communities, and society as a whole.

Continual data-driven adjustments are the cornerstone of successful homelessness initiatives. By analyzing data and making informed changes, programs can adapt to the evolving needs of the homeless population, ensuring long-term effectiveness. Let's delve into some examples of how data-driven adjustments have made a significant impact on homelessness initiatives.

Seattle's Navigation Center:

In Seattle, the Navigation Center was established as a response to the growing homelessness crisis. By collecting and analyzing data on the demographics and needs of individuals seeking shelter, the center was able to tailor its services accordingly. **Through data-driven insights**, they discovered that many homeless individuals had pets, which served as a barrier to accessing traditional shelters. As a result, the Navigation Center implemented pet-friendly policies, leading to increased engagement and trust among this vulnerable population.

Los Angeles' Coordinated Entry System:

In Los Angeles, the Coordinated Entry System was developed to streamline access to housing resources for homeless individuals. **Data analysis** revealed that certain groups, such as veterans or families with children, faced unique challenges in finding suitable housing. In response, the system was adjusted to prioritize these groups for housing placements, leading to quicker exits from homelessness and more targeted support services.

Salt Lake City's Housing First Initiative:

Salt Lake City's Housing First Initiative is a prime example of the power of data-driven adjustments. By closely monitoring outcomes and tracking progress, city officials were able to identify areas for improvement within the program. **Through careful analysis of data**, they found that additional support services, such as mental health counseling and job training, were needed to ensure long-term housing stability for participants. By integrating these services into the initiative, success rates improved significantly.

San Francisco's Homeward Bound Program:

San Francisco's Homeward Bound Program utilizes data analytics to identify trends and patterns among homeless individuals seeking reunification with family or friends outside the city. **By leveraging data insights**, program coordinators were able to optimize travel arrangements, provide necessary documentation assistance, and offer ongoing support post-reunification. This tailored approach resulted in higher success rates and strengthened relationships with partnering organizations.

The Mississippi Gulf Coast Housing First Coordinated Entry Initiative

The Mississippi Gulf Coast's approach to addressing homelessness serves as a powerful example of how the strategic use of data, combined with community collaboration, can make substantial and lasting impacts. Following the devastation of Hurricane Katrina in 2005, the region faced an overwhelming crisis, with over seven hundred (700) individuals experiencing homelessness in the lower six counties of the state. The situation was dire, with housing destroyed, and many people displaced with limited resources to rebuild their lives. However, 20 years later, the landscape of homelessness in the area looks remarkably different, with the January 2024 Point-in-Time (PIT) Count recording only 154 unsheltered individuals.

The reduction in homelessness on the Mississippi Gulf Coast is no coincidence. It can be largely credited to the leadership of the Open Doors Homeless Coalition, the Collaborative Applicant and HMIS Lead Agency for MS-503, which was and continues to be responsible for organizing the efforts associated with reductions in homelessness and ensuring housing stability and permanent housing destinations for the individuals and family beneficiaries, and its two Executive Directors, Mary Simons and Dena Wittmann. Under their guidance, they established a dynamic and adaptable network of collaboration among nonprofit organizations, government agencies, and service providers. Open Doors Homeless Coalition functioned as the central hub, with each partner organization functioning as a spoke, contributing its unique expertise, skills, and resources therefore providing a more holistic approach to those persons experiencing homelessness. This collective effort transformed a shared vision into a powerful force for change. By integrating data-driven strategies, focusing on prevention, and implementing a no-wrong-door approach, the region has made substantial progress in reducing homelessness.

Open Doors and Collaborative Leadership

At the heart of this transformation is the leadership of Open Doors Homeless Coalition, which spearheaded the region's Housing First Coordinated Entry Initiative. This system ensured that individuals experiencing homelessness were connected to the appropriate resources through a streamlined, coordinated process. Open Doors played a pivotal role in forming partnerships with local nonprofits such as Climb CDC, Back Bay Mission, Sue's Home, Hancock County Resource Center, Center for Nonviolence, Gulf Coast Mental Health Association, and Coastal Family Health Centers, among others. These organizations, each with their unique missions, have been essential in creating a holistic safety net for individuals and families at risk of or experiencing homelessness.

By coordinating these partnerships and fostering collaboration across sectors, Open Doors was able to break down the silos that traditionally hindered progress. This collaborative spirit also allowed for the implementation of diverse housing solutions that addressed specific needs, including Permanent Supportive Housing for those experiencing chronic homelessness, specialized housing for Veterans, and tailored support for youth and young adults facing unstable housing conditions.

Data-Driven Solutions and Tailored Housing Programs

The region's success has also been driven by its commitment to data. By tracking and analyzing homelessness data consistently, the Mississippi Gulf Coast has been able to identify trends, address gaps in service, refine its approach, and streamline processes to make them more accessible and manageable by those in need and the staff of the collaborating agencies. The Point-in-Time Counts, annual surveys that provide a snapshot of homelessness in the region, have been crucial for assessing the effectiveness of interventions and making necessary adjustments.

For example, data showed that Veterans and those experiencing chronic homelessness required specialized interventions. As a result, programs like the Veterans Affairs Supportive Housing (VASH) were expanded, offering Veterans permanent housing coupled with supportive services. Similarly, the region's Permanent Supportive Housing (PSH) programs targeted those with long-term homelessness and complex medical and mental health needs. These housing-first strategies were implemented with the understanding that stable housing is the foundational step toward resolving homelessness for these populations.

The Path to Functional Zero

Over the past ten years, the Mississippi Gulf Coast has achieved Functional Zero for Veterans, chronic homelessness, family homelessness, and youth homelessness. Reaching Functional Zero means that homelessness is rare, brief, and non-recurring, as the region has built a system that can effectively prevent and resolve homelessness when it occurs. This success story underscores the importance of prevention activities, such as outreach efforts, and the coordinated entry system that connects people to housing resources more efficiently using non-traditional methodologies.

The no-wrong-door coordinated entry system ensures that individuals seeking help can enter through any agency and be connected to the appropriate services. By minimizing barriers to access, the Gulf Coast has been able to reduce the number of people experiencing unsheltered homelessness, ensuring that once housed, individuals remain stably housed through continued supportive wraparound services, thereby to use a medical metaphor, treating the whole person and not simply the symptom.

A Blueprint for Long-Term Success

The success of the Mississippi Gulf Coast serves as a critical lesson in how community collaboration, data-driven approaches, and a coordinated entry system can lead to lasting solutions for homelessness. By investing in both prevention and tailored housing programs, and by fostering strong partnerships, the region has demonstrated that ending homelessness is not just an idealistic goal—it is an attainable reality.

The leadership of Mary Simons and Dena Wittmann at Open Doors has been essential to this progress, and their ability to mobilize resources and unite organizations around a common goal continues to inspire efforts nationwide. As the numbers of unsheltered individuals continue to decrease in the region, the Mississippi Gulf Coast stands as a testament to the power of data, collaboration, flexibility to respond, and commitment in tackling one of America's most pressing social issues.

With sustained efforts and continued partnerships, this model of success can be replicated and refined to meet the unique needs of other communities across the country. Passion alone will not achieve such results but will ultimately end in disappointment and burnout. The keys to achieving such results are collaboration and flexibility. Ending homelessness by 2035 requires the same level of dedication and intentionality that the Mississippi Gulf Coast has displayed—proving that with the right strategies, solutions are within reach.

Conclusion:

Data-driven adjustments are not only beneficial but essential in addressing homelessness effectively. By continuously evaluating programs, identifying areas for improvement through data analysis, and implementing targeted changes based on empirical evidence, initiatives can adapt to meet the diverse needs of homeless populations. These examples demonstrate the tangible impact of making informed adjustments in homelessness strategies, paving the way for sustainable solutions that lead to long-term success in combating homelessness.

The journey towards eradicating homelessness in America by 2035 is complex, yet attainable with the right tools and strategies at our disposal. The pivotal role of data in this process cannot be overstated. By monitoring and adjusting homelessness strategies through rigorous data analysis, we ensure that our actions are not just hopeful endeavors but are backed by empirical evidence and tailored to meet the evolving needs of the population.

Data serves as the compass that guides our efforts, helping to pinpoint which initiatives are effective and which require refinement. As we've explored throughout this chapter, the dynamic nature of homelessness demands that our strategies adapt continually. This adaptability is only possible when grounded in robust data collection and analysis frameworks. Through examples of successful data-driven adjustments, we have seen firsthand how such approaches can significantly enhance the effectiveness of homelessness initiatives.

The process of making informed adjustments based on data is integral to achieving long-term success. It ensures that resources are utilized efficiently and that interventions are responsive to the real-time dynamics of homelessness. This approach does not merely react to the symptoms of homelessness but strategically addresses its underlying causes, paving the way for sustainable solutions.

The overarching goal of this book has been to provide a clear, actionable, and comprehensive plan to systematically address and ultimately eradicate homelessness in America. By integrating the insights from each chapter, including the critical importance of data-driven decision-making showcased here, we equip policymakers, activists, and concerned citizens with a roadmap that is both practical and adaptable.

Through this detailed yet approachable guide, stakeholders are empowered to not only understand the systemic issues contributing to homelessness but also to actively participate in crafting solutions that are informed by data and characterized by continual improvement. This ensures that our strategies are not static but evolve alongside the changing landscapes of our communities.

By harnessing the power of data, we foster a culture of precision and accountability in our fight against homelessness. This approach does not merely aim to manage the issue temporarily but seeks to resolve it permanently by 2035. The commitment to data-driven strategies highlighted in this chapter underscores a fundamental truth: *knowledge is power*. Armed with the right information, and continually refining our methods based on that information, we stand a much stronger chance of transforming the ideal of ending homelessness into a reality.

Let us move forward with the confidence that our efforts are guided by clarity and driven by evidence. Together, let us build a future where homelessness is not just managed, but ended—a testament to what can be achieved when we combine compassion with innovation and data-driven precision.

Epilogue

A Vision Fulfilled: Ending Homelessness by 2035

As we draw the curtains on our exploration and blueprint for eradicating homelessness, let's pause and reflect on the journey we've undertaken together. Throughout this book, we've dissected the intricacies of homelessness, a pervasive issue that touches every corner of America, unraveling its complex layers and proposing actionable solutions.

We've mapped out a path that isn't just hopeful but is embedded in practicality and driven by community engagement and informed policy-making. This blueprint isn't merely a plan but a call to action for each one of us—policymakers, community leaders, activists, and socially-conscious citizens—to ignite change in our respective spheres.

Imagine the ripple effect when these strategies are implemented across communities: local governments adopting more inclusive zoning laws, businesses providing job opportunities to the homeless, healthcare institutions ensuring accessible mental health services, and schools educating young minds about social responsibility.

By integrating the strategies discussed—ranging from housing-first approaches to multi-sector collaboration and sustainable funding models—you have the power to transform abstract ideas into concrete results. This book is your toolkit; each chapter equips you with knowledge to understand and tackle different facets of homelessness. Whether you're drafting policy, organizing community support, or simply educating others, you're now armed with a comprehensive understanding of what it takes to make a significant impact.

However, it's crucial to recognize the limitations within our current scope. Our strategies might require adaptation to fit diverse community needs and unforeseen economic conditions. Thus, continual research and adaptation are key components in our ongoing battle against homelessness.

Take this knowledge beyond the pages. Start conversations, challenge outdated policies, participate in community planning meetings, or volunteer your time. Each small action contributes to a larger change.

As we conclude this discussion, remember that ending homelessness by 2035 is an ambitious yet achievable goal. It requires perseverance, collaboration, and, most importantly, a unified belief in the dignity of every individual. Let us step forward with determination and hope.

In closing, let's recall the words of Helen Keller: "Alone we can do so little; together we can do so much." This sentiment resonates deeply with our mission—a collective effort is paramount to turning the tide against homelessness. Let us be united in this cause and inspired by our shared humanity to create lasting change.

Let's make this vision a reality. Together, we can end homelessness.